WHO ARE YOU?

The art of
being yourself
in a world
full of masks...

Jamie Naegele

Published by
Hasmark Publishing International
www.hasmarkpublishing.com

First Edition

Editor: Jamie Schelz
jamieschelz@hasmarkpublishing.com

Cover and Book Design: Anne Karklins, Kelly Kinsman
anne@hasmarkpublishing.com

ISBN 13: 978-1-989756-16-4
ISBN 10: 1989756166

This book is dedicated to all the people who feel they are missing something in their lives. I sincerely believe that you will find it. I hope this book will help.

Contents

Acknowledgments

Many people have had a tremendous impact on my life, too many to acknowledge here. But I automatically fail if I never try, so I will give it a shot. I first want to thank you, the reader, for investing in yourself to help better your life. For this, I promise to give my absolute best to provide you with as many tools, tricks and tips that I can so you can apply this information to your daily lives. Because, after all, it is for you that I am writing this book.

Then of course there is my best friend, who has always been there for me, even in my darkest of times. She was the real catalyst in changing my life around, and she taught me what true friendship looks like. I know our friendship has been rocky, as most great friendships are, but we have always been able to be there for each other, especially when it matters most. For this, I am truly grateful. I love you, my dear friend.

I want to thank my Momma for always loving my brother and me "the purplest." The sacrifices she has made for us show me the real power love can have. She is a shining example of how to bounce back from adversity and keep going. Most people could not have done all that she has done and be where she is today. I would say that I am proud of her, but I know that she is proud of herself, which in this world is all that really matters. She has always tried to challenge me, to encourage me to be a better version of myself than I currently am. But, more importantly, she has always driven home the moral of doing the right thing. With infamous examples such as "the square peg in a round hole," I can proudly say she is someone who has taught me these values. I love you, Momma.

My Dad has always been there for me, especially when I needed him the most. I cannot thank him enough for giving me the opportunity to find my passion. He has shown me endless support in this journey called life, but what I am truly grateful for are the values he has instilled in me. All of his classic lines —"Take care of the little things, and the big things will take care of themselves," "Love is an action, it is what we do that truly counts," "Always remember the value in Random Acts of Kindness"— will always resonate with me. I love you, Dad.

My not-so-little brother has always been the first one to point out when something is wrong in my thinking, and then shows me a better way to look at things. He always stands up for what he believes in, a trait that sometimes gets lost in a world that tilts toward conformity. I wasn't always a good brother growing up, but I hope to be now. I want to encourage him to keep learning, even after school, picking subjects that he enjoys and can help him grow as a person. However, if he does nothing else, I hope he chooses a life that makes him happy, however he defines happiness. Happiness, ultimately, is what life is all about. I love you, bro-da-man. Always be you.

My Grandma has been the glue that has kept our wonderful family together. She was always by my Grandpa's side until the very end, clearly making his life much happier because of it. I also have to thank her and my extended family for putting up with all of our recent Thanksgiving shenanigans—and still loving us anyway. It's never a dull moment when you are with the Naegeles, and keeping an open mind is always a part of that. I love you, Grandma.

I have to thank my cousins for taking the photographs for the cover design, but also for choosing to remain a part of our family. They could have easily chose to leave, and I am so grateful that they didn't. I am especially thankful for the two boys they have so wonderfully raised (which includes you, Aunt). The boys are both geniuses in their own unique way and clearly will be successful in whatever they do, however they define success. I love all of you.

To all the people who rejected me in my times of loneliness, I must thank you. If you hadn't rejected me, I would not have continued to grow. My life would not have been on the same path it is today. Although it stung in the moment, I can look back and be extremely grateful it happened the way it did. For this, I love you all.

Lastly, I have to thank the woman who helped inspire me to continue writing this book. I will always love you with all of my heart. Always remember: Have Fun, Learn Stuff, Help Others.

To all of you, I thank you from the most honest part of my soul. Without all of you, my life would not be the same.

Preface

"The search for happiness is one of the chief sources of unhappiness."

– Eric Hoffer, Philosopher

I was looking for it. I thought I would find it if I moved across the country. I bought a house at 24, thinking it had to be there. It wasn't. I sold my house for $40,000 more than I paid for it, and I moved back home. With all of this new cash, I thought it would be back home, waiting for me all along. It wasn't there either! So I bought a brand new car — it had to be in there, right? I heard you lose 20% of a new car's value when you drive it off the lot, but that really doesn't matter as long as I have it! I didn't find it in there either! Would I ever find it? Or would I be searching for it my entire life? I'm talking, of course, about happiness. I was looking on the outside for an emotion that happens on the inside. Ironic, isn't it?

On the outside, I had everything a young man should need to be happy: a new car, a high-paying job, a cute girlfriend, and a nice apartment. What's not to be happy about? Except I wasn't. I was actually miserable. So in March of 2019, I decided I was going to find happiness. Damn was I wrong. Happiness isn't something I had to find; happiness is something I had to create.

What is your definition of happiness? Most people can't define happiness, and because they can't define what makes them happy, they look for it instead. But defining happiness is like defining the word green. You can say things like green is a color that looks like grass or emeralds, and you can say that happiness is an emotion that feels like joy or contentment. But you can't see green or feel happiness through words. So, instead of defining what these words are, let's explain how we create them.

Green is the art of mixing blue and yellow. Happiness is the art of being yourself. True happiness comes from a feeling of love. It comes when we spend time with the people who make us feel loved, and when we work at a job we love. But mostly, it comes when we love *ourselves*. Because if we do not fully love ourselves, then our moment to moment happiness becomes dependent on having to be around people who make us feel loved, or working at a job that we are in love with — which not everyone has the luxury of experiencing every moment of every day, or even at all. But happiness is not meant to be dependent on the outside world. Happiness is meant to be habitual in our inside world.

Habitual happiness comes from habitually loving yourself, or else it becomes dependent on things outside your control. But in order to love yourself, you must be yourself. Otherwise, who are you actually loving?

People always tell us that loving ourselves is important, but no one has ever really told us how—or even what that would look like. It's almost impossible to get somewhere if you don't have a road map or even a clue about what your destination looks like. And we've all heard that advice before: "Just be yourself! You'll get the job if you just be yourself! He/She will like you if you just be yourself!" Without defining what "Be Yourself" really means, it can be very ambiguous advice. That's because in order to be yourself, you must first know *who you are.*

Who are you? The answer to this question is actually quite simple, and yet unique for every single person on this planet. In almost every interaction you have with another person, they are asking you this question. They probably won't ask you directly, but they'll ask you questions such as "Where are you from? What do you do for work? What do you do for fun?" These questions are designed to get to know you, to find out: Who are you, really?

This book is crafted to help you find — or maybe to create — the happiness most people seem to be searching for, to finally see who you truly are, and most importantly to BE who you truly are. Because the goal of life is to sustain happiness — not to always be chasing it.

If you want to get the most out of this book, please remember: *Applied* knowledge is power. Power is change. Knowledge is useless if it isn't applied. Some people read books for inspiration. They read books to feel better, and then once they feel that moment of inspiration they forget to apply the information they just learned. If you read just for inspiration without applying what you have learned, you become an encyclopedia for other people to improve their lives, without ever improving your own.

So don't just read: do. Don't just think: act. I tried to provide as many examples as I could so you can use these concepts with your imagination to see how they can be applied to your own life. Personally, I read books with a highlighter, highlighting the important information that I think can improve my life. That way I can go back and take notes or reread information I want to stick with me. I encourage you to do the same if this technique works for you.

Let this book be your road map — your guiding light to being yourself, loving yourself, and enjoying the blissful peace of habitual happiness. Let's show the world who we truly are, and the happiness that comes from simply being ourselves.

CHAPTER ONE

The Night I Figured It Out

"I always liked those moments of epiphany, when you have the next destination."

– Brad Pitt, Actor

Last October, I went to a party that was hosted by someone I had recently met. I hadn't been to a party in quite some time because I was on a new path in my life. I was what most people would call a "loner." Of course, I would prefer the term "Lone Wolf." It has a better ring to it: more badass, and less like I'm a hitchhiker serial killer. Plus, while loners tend to drift around, Lone Wolves know where they're going, and I knew the direction I was headed—or so I thought.

Being a Lone Wolf was actually very new for me. I had always been a social butterfly, especially in college. I was in a fraternity, and I considered everyone to be my friend. I also had many friends in other fraternities, which gave me an entry into most parties. It was really easy to make friends back then: a tap to the nose and a hand in my pocket—a gesture that means "I have drugs; wanna do some?"—made me welcomed anywhere. That was a particularly ugly time in my life, but one that can only be seen in the rearview mirror. For me, it wasn't so much the drugs, but it was the feeling of sharing in an area where most people wouldn't. It was an easy way to stand out, and for people to think "This kid's cool."

Most of my friendships revolved around drinking. I had somewhat of a drinking problem. It wasn't that I always had to drink, but that I never knew when to stop. It led me to make many mistakes — all of which have made me into the person I am today. The beautiful thing about my story is that if I can change, anyone can. That may sound like a cliché, but if you had met me ten years ago, six years ago, or even a year ago, you would never recognize me. I began last year borderline obese, depressed and severely insecure. I had the choice to keep living a life I wasn't meant for or to create a life worth living. I chose the latter. And in the process, I have discovered what can make us all truly happy. No matter where we are or what kind of person we are, we can always improve our life.

The party that I mentioned earlier was definitely going to be a party of mostly people I hadn't met before. As I arrived, I recognized a familiar face that I wasn't expecting to see. It was an old college buddy I hadn't talked to in a while. I was hoping to have a deep, meaningful conversation with him — the kind most people aren't used to having. Small talk bores the hell out of me, and I like to talk about ideas, especially ones that can help us improve each other's lives.

As I tried to discuss the power of choices with him, I noticed that he was feeling uncomfortable, so I changed the subject to a less deep, empowering idea. I've come to realize that some people need to be eased into talking about ideas.

In the midst of our conversation, somehow the topic of salmon came up. It felt like he was looking for a way to change the conversation. He went on a fifteen-minute rant about his love of salmon—all the ways you can cook and eat it. I felt like I was in a scene from *Forrest Gump*, except that we were talking about salmon instead of shrimp. So there I was, hearing about this man's love for salmon, thinking to myself, "This is why I am a Lone Wolf right now."

As the night went on, the party started to draw back memories from old college experiences. From funneling Four Lokos to endless nights of beer pong, I remembered how I used to behave at parties.

I always felt the need to impress people by trying to prove how awesome my alcohol tolerance was. Always moving past the point of having fun to making myself look completely foolish in front of everyone. It was like I was remembering a younger, different version of myself, but also feeling a sense of gratitude for the lessons life has taught me.

Later in the night when most people had left the party, a few had remained. As I was trying to figure out my next move, I found myself listening to a political conversation between a Democrat and a Republican. I purposely do not know a lot about politics. Every conversation about politics seems to agitate people—even if they agree with each other.

So, as this political discussion started, I wondered where it would go. Would this be a civil conversation or more like an episode of *Jerry Springer?*

When I hear most people talk about current politics, it usually ends with the Democrat saying "Screw Donald Trump!" and the Republican replying "Screw you!" To my surprise, it was very relaxed because they were both explaining their own viewpoints, respecting the other's and agreeing to disagree. Both parties just want what is best for the country; they just have different ideas about what measures will accomplish that.

After the conversation ended, I decided to ride share to a local bar that I had never been to. It was around midnight, and the bar was closing at 3 a.m. Inside the bar is a huge area with a large dance floor to the left and an outdoor patio to the right. Between them was the indoor bar where people got their drinks. When I entered, I decided to go toward the dance floor — and I was surprised to see that there was another indoor bar in its own little corner of that room.

As I went to get a drink, I noticed two of my old fraternity brothers were there. I was actually pretty excited to see them. They were older than me, and I had looked up to them back in the day. They were definitely the "jock" type: athletic, funny and good dudes to party with. As I greeted them, one seemed surprised and happy to see me. The other one gave me that look that said, "Okay, you saw me. Hello. Now please go away." I went to get a drink, and they left the bar shortly after.

Surprisingly, the encounter didn't bother me too much. If it had been a year or two earlier, it certainly would have. But I have come to learn that when people reject me, they are most likely doing me a favor. It can sting in the moment, but it always helps in the long run. As Jay Shetty always says, "Rejection is just redirection." If I were to see him again now, I would know to either say "Hello" and keep walking or to ignore him completely, wishing him happiness from a distance.

As it turns out, I was right. It actually was a blessing in disguise, because I was redirected to something better. If I had stayed and partied with them that night, I might not have figured out what has since completely changed my life.

As the night went on, I found myself outside alone on the patio, the only quiet area, staring into the night sky. Inside the bar there was loud, blasting music that made everyone's conversation sound like "What?! Huh?! I can't really hear you. Isn't this fun?!"

Eventually, I walked back into the bar and headed toward the dance floor. Most people were dancing without a care in the world. Others were crowded into circles, being slightly insecure about their dance moves. At that point I just stood there and asked myself, "Why are people here? Why do people keep coming to these loud bars almost every weekend, getting hammered and probably waking up with a hangover and maybe even some late-night regrets?"

I understood it when I was in college. Everyone around me was partying, and hangovers seemed to be nonexistent. I could drink the bar out of business with my friends one night, and wake up the next morning like nothing ever happened. Spring right up out of bed, possibly the floor, still slightly drunk, thinking, "Whoa. What happened? Let's do it again!" These days, if I've had as little as two different kinds of beer, I wake up like *Spongebob* leaving the ocean.

So as I stood there at the edge of the dance floor, watching people of all different ages dancing the night away, I pondered these questions. Then I realized that I was actually asking these questions about myself. Why am I here? Why do I keep coming to these places and getting hammered? And finally, in an instant, I got an answer. It was like someone turned on the light switch too fast and the bulb shattered, or more like the exploding-head emoji, but with a smile on my face. In that instant, I realized I was there trying to find what almost everyone is looking for: *approval.*

Approval? How do I get that from a bunch of drunk people dancing to loud music? And how does that apply to everyone, and what people are looking for? These were the questions I then started to ask myself. As I thought about the answer I had received, I realized why my life had been so depressing before, and why I was so happy now.

If the word *approval* doesn't seem like the key to happiness, that could be a matter of language. Unless we were a spelling-bee contestant, most of us arrive at the definitions of words not from dictionaries but from conversations. Every person's sense of the meaning of words may be subjective, flexible, allowing differences of interpretation in different contexts. So, the way in which I understand approval may be different from the way you do, or we just have different connotations.

Continue reading, and I will show you how happiness comes from approval.

CHAPTER TWO

The Cycle of Approval

"What the superior man seeks is in himself, what the small man seeks is in others."

– Confucius, Ancient Chinese Philosopher

At its simplest, *approval* means the acceptance of behaviors and opinions of others, whether from an individual or an entire group. People don't crave approval only when they are insecure. There is a biological need for approval deeply rooted within every one of us. In tribal societies, people who are disapproved of or rejected by the group are often banished from the community — sent into exile. So in the tribal stages of our human development, rejected members might have been left out in the wild with no help to hunt, fish or find shelter. In other words, in mankind's tribal periods, being rejected by the group brought the fear of death.

You can still see evidence of that need for approval in most human interactions today. You can see it in the child who craves parental attention. You can see it in the teenager who decides to do drugs to seem "cool"— despite knowing it's a bad idea. You can see it when people lie to protect themselves from possible rejection by their peers. And it's painfully obvious to see it when people try to be someone they are not, to fit into a group where they do not belong.

As children, we first seek approval from our family members. We want our parents and our older siblings to approve of our behavior. If they do not, we may be punished. It's essentially a game of learning what is acceptable behavior in the eyes of the family tribe. If I cry, do they pay more attention to me? If I help around the house or say something nice to someone, do I get praise? Or does it get brushed off as if nothing happened? If I act up and lash out, will they give me what I want, or will I get in trouble? As we get older, we begin to learn how and how not to behave. This is why some children turn out bratty and others are deemed to be well-behaved. We learn our behaviors through a sequence of approvals and rejections.

For most of us, things start to get really weird when we are teenagers. It's a time when hormones start to change, and it's a time when we start seeking the approval of our friends and classmates. Sometimes our friends may try to peer pressure us to do things we know we shouldn't. If, for whatever reason, our friends think that huffing paint is cool, we may join in to seem cool, too. Likewise, if our friend base likes to play video games and/or sports, we most likely will be heavily involved in those activities as well.

It is in our teenage years that this need for approval becomes more intense. We are introduced to comprehend a world beyond our family. We try to blend in with the crowd, hoping to gain the approval of our peers. Unfortunately, that approval doesn't always come easily, because instead of teaching us to be kind to one another, most school systems create an environment based on competition.

Our education system ranks students' intelligence and takes other measures to predict their success in life, mostly based on grades. As a result, society tends to view "smarter" students as better than the rest. This gives "A" students a sense of high self-esteem. But what about the "B" students? Or even the "C" students? Do they have high self-esteem if they think other students are better than them?

Deep down, we all know that we all are created equal. We may not all be born on an equal playing field in the game of life, but we all innately know that no one person is better than another. It's even written in our Declaration of Independence:

> *"We hold these truths to be self-evident, that all men are created equal, that they are endowed by their Creator with certain unalienable Rights, that among these are Life, Liberty, and the pursuit of Happiness."*
>
> – Thomas Jefferson, Declaration of Independence

So when society begins to view one child as "better" than another child, based on measures such as perceived intelligence, children instinctively know this isn't true. Or at least they do not want it to *feel* true. So in order to level the playing field and increase their self-esteem, children start to bully one another. The "B" and "C" students call the "A" students nerds. The "A" students call the "B" and "C" students dumb. The "B" students call the "C" students stupid. When everyone seems to be bullying and rejecting everyone, the need for approval becomes intense —which creates what I call "the cycle of approval." In a world full of rejections, the cycle for the need for approval has now begun.

Think back to when you were in high school or even middle

school. Were you ever made fun of for anything? Even if it wasn't consistently or considered just a joke, any feeling of rejection (especially if it's something you cannot control), at such an early age can create a lasting sense of fear.

In the new age of the internet, the bullying doesn't stop at school. With the web, students have endless knowledge at their fingertips. So, they use the internet in new ways to bully each other to boost their own self-esteem.

There are two ways to boost our self-esteem: by building ourselves up or by tearing others down. The first way is dependent on making a comparison of our current self with who we were before. The second way is dependent on comparing ourselves with other people. When we compare our current self to our former self, other people can't affect our self-esteem negatively — they aren't even in the equation. But when comparing ourselves to other people, our self-esteem is reliant on feeling better than them. And when people tear us down, it can only feel right to tear others down too, to enhance our self-esteem.

So when our education system compares some students to other students' disadvantages, those students may feel compelled to even the score. They create insulting memes. They make embarrassing videos. They do everything they can to boost their self-esteem, even if it's only temporarily. Then, once someone bullies them, they are left to find a new way to boost their self-esteem — to go bully someone else.

If we aren't bullied about our grades, we get bullied for something else. It could be the way we dress, our physical appearance, our hobbies and interests, our athletic abilities or anything else that doesn't make us seem to "fit in." So then the safe zone becomes to stay within the crowd and to not stand out, for fear we will get bullied. This impulse to "stay in the crowd" can sometimes follow us for the rest of our lives.

Our teenage years are some of our most formative. It's when

we make the transition from being parent-dependent to being friend-dependent. It's when we begin to venture off on our own, to explore and then decide who we truly are. So then the effect of this constant bullying as we progress through life creates fear, anxiety and the habitual behavior of comparing ourselves to others.

This fear causes some people to become afraid to succeed, afraid to fail or to become afraid of being anything different from the crowd. It can also cause anxiety about what other people might think about the decisions we make. Fear and anxiety are paralyzing. They cause us to remain the same, to avoid standing out from the crowd and to not be our true, authentic selves. Fear makes us irrational, often causing us to make choices that we wouldn't have made otherwise. This is the result of the cycle of bullying: people rejecting other people for who they are if they act any different from the crowd.

When we try to fit in, or pretend to be someone we are not, it leaves us wearing a mask. These masks prevent us from being who we truly are. They cause us to keep looking for the approval of others to prevent us from the feeling of rejection. The masks also cause us to do things we normally wouldn't do.

When I was in high school, my first mask could be seen as a chubby, immature "know-it-all" whose role model was Eric Cartman from the show *South Park*. If you know the TV show, you know that he's the little fat kid who insults others ruthlessly. Unfortunately, Cartman was who I aspired to be. I even tried talking and sounding like him. I prided myself on being witty, making sure that anyone who made fun of me would regret it. I would take things to the extreme, even to the point where people wanted to fight me. I was just a kid, but a kid whose self-esteem was dependent on tearing other people down.

The only reason I bullied anyone else was because deep down

I was hurting, deep down I was insecure. I was a bully because I was always bullied. Growing up, I was constantly made fun of for two things: being chubby and not being able to talk to girls. In December of my senior year of high school, I looked at my stomach. Playing with my big old belly, I thought to myself, "I am *done* being fat." I made a conscious decision then and there to lose weight. I ordered P90X and began working out almost every day. I also completely changed my diet. I cut out anything that had any fat in it at all. (I had no idea what I what was doing; healthy fat is good for us and vital for optimal health). For lunch, instead of the fatty foods I usually got at school, like pizza and burgers, I went with a bland deli sandwich every single day. The result? After three months, I had lost more than forty pounds. I was in the absolute best shape of my life. I had a sense of self-worth and self-esteem that I never knew existed. And you know what happened after that? I still was made fun of. People started to call me P90X, more to put me down than in saying "nice job." They thought it was funny that I even had to work out in the first place. Whenever Facebook photos of me were posted, someone would immediately tag "P90X" on my stomach. It bothered me, but not nearly as much as being fat did.

It was soon after I had lost weight that I started going to parties. With this new sense of confidence, I was able to talk to girls without having to keep my head down. And then I finally kissed a girl! A full on make-out session. I thought the teasing would finally stop, but it didn't. I still was made fun of. People thought it was hilarious that I was now trying to talk to girls. From then on, I was accused of "going on the prowl." "Naegele's on the prowl!" people chanted when they saw me in the hallway.

Why? Why did people continue making fun of me when I had made a 180-degree change? Because my behavior hadn't changed. I still acted like a bully. I still made fun of other people. Treating others the way we want to be treated isn't just a cute saying, or even a guideline to follow. It is a fact of life. Treat others the way we want to be treated because that is *exactly* how they are going to treat us. If we treat people with hate, selfishness and arrogance, that is how they are going to treat us. If we treat people with kindness, generosity and compassion, that is how they are going to treat us. Even if a particular person does not, someone else will, because energy always comes back to its point of origin, and kindness is the best energy there is.

As you will find out later in this book, kindness is a skill we can all learn. You can teach someone how to be kind to others. But unfortunately, our education system doesn't teach us that — at least not successfully. It indirectly teaches us how to compete with one another. So in the midst of this competition, instead of being kind, we rank each other. We judge each other about things like attractiveness, status, intelligence, popularity and wealth.

That is why not all approval is created equal. There are really only two elements that come into play when we seek others' approval. I call one of them "the frame" and the other one "the prestige." The frame is the way we see or compare someone else in relation to ourselves. Are they prettier, stronger, wealthier or more popular? Or is it vice-versa?

The prestige is how we rank or value other people. Most people adopt what society calls "prestige"; they value money, fame, and status the most. When we are in the cycle of approval, we tend to want the approval of people we frame as a much higher prestige than us more than we do others—which is why so many people want the attention of celebrities. Also in this cycle of approval, we don't need the approval from the people we frame as having what we consider lower prestige than ours. We assume we've already got it. We view them as lower, so they must approve of us regardless — which is why some people can act so snobby.

So instead of dropping comparisons, we try to bolster our own prestige so that we can receive more approval from others. We work at jobs we hate. We buy things to impress people we don't like, usually with money that we don't have. We follow the latest fashion trends, trying to keep up with what people in the celebrity world wear—regardless of how uncomfortable that may be. Sometimes we even marry people not because we love them but because they're the perfect "trophy" spouse, or they have a lot of money. We do all of these things just to impress others. We want everyone to think our lives are perfect on the outside without focusing on what's on the inside. We do it simply because we want to be able to say, "I'm better than you, and I don't need your approval."

My most recent mask was the mask of "Pretend-Success Jamie." I worked at a job I was miserable at because I made a lot of money, and it made me look "successful" as a young adult. The dress code included clothes that I would never wear otherwise, making me feel like an imposter right from the start. It was a typical desk job within an uncomfortable, stuffy office environment. I always felt as if I were walking on eggshells, that every word that came out of my mouth had the potential to get me fired. I constantly felt as if I wasn't good enough for the position, and my ability to speak up confidently was at an all-time low. This wasn't the company's fault. It was my decision to wear what everyone else wore, to choose a position that required me to sit at a desk, choosing to fear other people's opinions. This was the result of wearing a mask that hid who I was from the rest of the office. In my head, their disapproval would mean an end to my "success." I was afraid to get fired from a job I didn't want because I wanted to "look" successful.

The job paid a lot, which is another reason I was afraid to get fired. With more income but no money skills, came the freedom to spend a lot of money to look and feel like I was in the luxury class. I had an expensive apartment, bought a new car off the lot, and gathered as many unnecessary "things" as I could. Although all of my money consequently went to rent, the new car and other bills, I still needed a way to buy more stuff. But I was in luck! Since I had such a high income, I was able to get high-limit credit cards to "afford" all of my new toys. As I tried to play the credit card game, I began to accumulate more and more debt.

At this point, not only did my debt start to grow — so did my belly again. In less than three years at this company, I gained almost eighty pounds. All of that hard work I had done to lose weight in high school was quickly swept away as I completely ignored my health in order to look "successful" in the eyes of others. In reality, I was just afraid of looking "unsuccessful."

As I continued going down this road of hating my life, taking it out on the people that mattered the most to me, and ignoring my health, I realized I couldn't live that way anymore. Something had to change.

So, in January of 2019, I quit my job to focus on my health and to figure out what I really wanted out of life. To answer the question, "Who am I, and why am I here?" This would eventually start the beginning of my "Lone Wolf" journey.

I saved my bonus, liquidated my 401k and began a process that has changed my life forever. I moved out of my expensive apartment and into my Dad's basement. I was in my mid-twenties, had no job, was living with my parents and weighed two hundred and forty pounds. To the outside world, I had gone five steps backwards. From my point of view, I had gone five steps deeper, so that I could go ten steps further.

Since then, I have lost over seventy pounds, have established multiple sources of income, and can honestly say that I am the happiest I have ever been in my entire life. And this only happened because I stopped focusing on other people's approval, and started to focus on my *own* approval.

True happiness comes from a feeling of love (this is why some people like dogs more than people). Like happiness, love is a hard word to define—or even understand. How would you define love? It's easier to define what love is not than what love is. Love is not mean or hurtful, and the feeling of love doesn't come when people are making fun of us, insulting us or making us feel rejected. So, if being rejected is not being loved, then does being approved of mean that we *are* loved?

A great example of this mentality would be women who are attracted to a type of man known as "the player." The player woos women over by playing the game of approval. They give a little approval out, and then they take it away — leaving the girl wanting more. The player gives back-handed compliments to leave the woman contemplating whether he really meant it as a compliment, or if it was just something negative that he was noticing. They do all of this enough times until the woman almost *needs* that approval from him. He plays the game until she has to win his approval in the form of sex, and then he drops her like a fly — leaving her to look for that feeling of love from someone new.

This example doesn't just apply to this type of woman. It applies to anyone who thinks they need approval from others to feel loved—which includes the player as well. The player thinks that having sex with lots of women makes him an "alpha male," and that sense of being an alpha male boosts his self-esteem because he feels better than other men who can't seem to get laid as often. The player is just as addicted to the cycle of approval as some of the women are—addicted to the false sense of love and happiness that approval brings. He also gets physical approval from "the game" in the form of sex, and once he gets that physical approval from one girl, it's on to the next.

On the way back from the bar on the night I figured out the cycle of approval, I had a deep conversation with the Uber driver. We got on the topic of sex, and he wanted to know why he always wanted to have sex with every pretty girl that he sees. He plays the game until he sleeps with her, and then wants nothing to do with her, and he couldn't figure out why he always did that. So I told him about what I had just learned that night, and that he was searching for approval. And once he got it from them, he didn't need it anymore. He said he didn't like that because it sounded needy, but he knew deep down that this was what he was doing. And the only way to stop the cycle of approval, is to switch from *whom* we are searching for approval from.

Happiness comes from a feeling that we are loved, but when we search for other people's approval for that feeling of love, our happiness then becomes conditional upon what other people think of us. When we search for the love of ourselves, when we approve of *ourselves*, our happiness becomes habitual because we approve of who we are, and we aren't afraid to show it. When we approve of ourselves, we don't need the approval of others. We are never seeking it from without; we already have it from within.

Have you ever noticed when you tell someone you are proud of them or praise them, and they sometimes brush it off with a simple "thank you" — as if it were nothing? That's because they don't need you to be proud of them; they are already proud of themselves.

A reverse example is a child seeking approval from their parents as they get older. One of the first things you hear is, "Mom, Dad, are you *proud* of me?" "Mom, I got good grades, are you proud of me?" "Dad, I hit a home run in today's game, are you proud of me?" These questions clearly indicate they are seeking their parents' approval. Most of the time the parent will respond with, "Great job! Keep up the good work!" But when parents say, "Keep up the good work," what the child hears is, "If you keep up the good work, I'll continue to stay proud of you.

I'll continue to *approve* of you." Parents don't recognize it in this way; they just want their kids to succeed in life. But what is more important — for their children to grow up to be successful, or for their children to grow up to be *happy*? When we do things for others to make them proud, we are looking for their approval. When we do things to make ourselves proud, we are looking for *our* approval.

Happiness comes from a feeling of love — or a feeling of approval. Habitual happiness comes from approving of ourselves. The only way to approve of ourselves — to love ourselves — is to *be* ourselves. Otherwise, who is it that we are actually loving? No one loves an ugly mask, especially the one wearing it.

So many people seem to be searching for happiness from the outside world, and that's because they believe that happiness comes from something external. But even when finding it here or there, it's only for a moment, followed shortly by wondering where it went and where to find it next. The reason such happiness comes and goes so quickly is because it is conditional. When happiness comes from somewhere outside of ourselves, we always need that external source to be happy.

Sometimes we seek happiness from drugs and alcohol. Drugs tend to give us a physical sense of happiness, meaning they create a rush of dopamine in the brain and sometimes what is known as a "body high." But that happiness is conditional on always having to be high to sustain it. I used to smoke marijuana regularly, starting at the age of seventeen. I was in love with the false sense of happiness that I thought it gave me. Most of the time, it would just make me paranoid, but I still wanted to chase that happy feeling. That happy feeling was conditional. It could only be sustained when I was high and quickly faded when I wasn't.

Marijuana can be a fantastic drug when used in the right way. It can help with certain medical conditions, help alleviate stress and even boost creativity from time to time. But when we rely on it for our happiness, it becomes a need instead of a tool.

Alcohol, on the other hand, lowers our inhibitions and causes us not to care what happens around us. That allows us to stop caring what other people think and to do whatever comes to mind. We seem to start to let ourselves be ourselves when we are drunk, which is why I think a lot of people like it so much. If we just learned to let go of our fears and still be ourselves without the alcohol, we wouldn't need it anymore. We could then use alcohol more as a tool to connect socially with friends, instead of as a need to sustain our happiness.

We may also tie our happiness to the people we surround ourselves with. If we need the people around us to make us feel happy, then our happiness is conditional on their approval. If they don't approve of us, then we aren't happy. This puts us in a box made up of what our friends will approve of and what they won't. But what if we have a falling out with a friend or our friendship group? Our happiness falls with it.

We may even tie our happiness to a false sense of cockiness, a feeling of being better than other people. When we have to feel "better" than other people to be happy, one negative comment about us can shatter our happiness. We lose the feeling of being better than everyone else, so we have to prove that we are. We may do things like tear others down, improve our social worth through high income jobs, sacrifice our health to become more attractive, and surround ourselves with people who make us look good—all to make ourselves feel better than everyone else, to have a false sense of happiness.

Sometimes we tend to think our happiness can be found somewhere new, in a place that isn't where we are now. Constantly looking for happiness in a new location means our happiness is conditional on always moving. I moved halfway across the country thinking I would find happiness. When I didn't find it after less than a year, I moved back home where I thought I would find it somewhere else. I didn't find it at home either—not until I figured out what true happiness is. It is not determined by my location, but created through my own approval.

All of these conditional states of happiness we chase are really just a false feeling of happiness. It can feel like happiness, but is it really? Or is it the happiness we have just settled for? Or is it just the only type of happiness we have been able to feel? It's happiness with strings attached; it's not going to last. Conditional happiness leaves us with the feeling that we are missing something, which causes us to continually chase it. Happiness isn't meant to come and go. True happiness is meant to be consistent, to last as long as we choose for it to.

The way to happiness can be defined as "the art of being yourself." If you want to be consistently happy, you always have to be yourself. If you really want to be yourself, then you have to act like yourself. And in order to act like yourself, you must first know *who you are.*

CHAPTER THREE

Who You Are

"To remember who you are, you must forget who they told you to be."

- Anonymous

Who are you? What do you tie your identity to? Are you your name or your body? Or are you just the accumulation of all the *things* you have? Or your occupation or your reputation? Are those who you are? Some people might answer yes to some of these questions. They attach their identity to the outside world. But if our identity is outside of us, then that means someone can take it away. People can call us an insulting name that is not our own. Our body can change in a moment or by an accident. All our things could get stolen from us. We could get fired or have our reputation ruined by one bad review. If this is what we attach our identity to, then our identity becomes outside of our control. Someone can take all of these things away from us at any moment. But who we are isn't something anyone outside of us can take away or change — unless we let them.

Who you are is simply the accumulation of *all* your beliefs. What makes every person unique is the different combination of the beliefs we all have. There are an infinite combination of beliefs, which is why no two people will ever be the same. You could have an identical twin and look exactly the same, but you would still have some beliefs that differentiate the two of you.

My definition of a belief is this: a thought or idea we hold about someone or something, or a concept that we think is true, whether it actually is or not. Most of us tend to believe that all of our beliefs are entirely true. Some people may even die for what they believe. But beliefs can be shattered in an instant.

Before 1954, it was believed that no one could ever run a four-minute mile. It just wasn't possible—your heart would explode if you tried. Then along came Roger Bannister. Roger Bannister broke the four-minute mile, proving to everyone that it *is* possible. Everyone who believed the four-minute mile was impossible had that belief shattered in an instant. But one thing is true: beliefs are something that no one can ever take away from you or change for you. Even if for most people, that specific belief got shattered in an instant, we can still choose to believe whatever it is that we want to believe.

Some people choose to believe in conspiracies, and we call them conspiracy theorists. Some people choose to believe that the earth is flat, and we call them flat-earthers. Every single person on the planet can choose whatever it is that they want to believe, and no one can ever take that away from them.

Although we are our beliefs, most of our beliefs haven't come from us. Most of them came from people we grew up with or surrounded ourselves with. And because they came from other people, are they really *ours*?

If you think to yourself that you aren't pretty enough, or you aren't good enough, or any other negative self-assessment, is it really *you* who believes that? Or is this critical voice inside your head actually someone else's? Is it your mom or your dad? Your friends or your siblings? Possibly a teacher who told you that you wouldn't be good at anything? Do you think that it is really you, the true you, who has any doubts about you?

It's likely that there is a difference between who you are today and who you are meant to be, or who you truly are. The true you loves everything about you. Every single person on the planet is born to love, but is taught to hate. This innate sense of love is especially true when it comes to loving ourselves. Babies are full of love and laughter. Yes, they may cry when they are hungry or tired, or to tell us they are lonely, but that's the only way they know how to get our attention. Otherwise, they are all smiles, giggles, and awe — learning what this beautiful world has to offer.

A toddler doesn't watch other people walking and think, "They can walk but I can't. They must be better than me." When babies see other people walking, they think, "If they can do it, so can I!" And then they try over and over until they do. As we grow older, the people around us tell us we are limited in certain ways. They tell us all the reasons that something's not possible. They set a standard of what can and can't be done, even if someone else has already achieved the same feat that we are assured we cannot also do. Society even tells us what "being attractive" is supposed to look like, and some people will tell us that we don't fit the bill. The limiting voice inside our head that says we aren't worthy, are incapable of success, are imperfect or not beautiful doesn't come from our true selves. It comes from the people and information we are surrounded by, from the time we are born until right now. All of our initial beliefs about the world come from the environment we were raised in.

There are two elements that determine how beliefs are formed:

an experience we have through our five senses and our reaction to that experience. Someone may tell you that you are ugly, which is something you hear. That might make you think, "I'm ugly? Really?" and a wave of insecurity can take over your emotions. Or you can think to yourself, "Ha! Nice one. I know I am beautiful!" and a wave of confidence takes over your emotions. This is how all of our beliefs, the things we think are true, get established: through an experience and our reaction to that experience. We can't always choose the experience, but beyond a certain age, we can always choose the reaction.

A puppy comes into this world believing that it can poop and pee wherever it wants to. But when we try to potty train our furry friends, we have to get them to change that belief, so that they then believe going to the bathroom inside is not okay. We reject the puppy's behavior for going inside, and it learns from our reaction that peeing on the carpet is a big no. We praise the puppy for going outdoors, and it learns that going potty outside is what is acceptable.

We humans learn in much the same way when we are youngsters, through a series of rejections and approvals of our behavior. These rejections and approvals form our beliefs about what is and isn't acceptable.

Our first set of beliefs is formed in the first six or seven years of our lives. Until the age of about seven, our brains have not yet developed in a way that allows us to choose the way we react to situations. The only way we know how to form reactions to experiences we encounter is to adopt the emotional reactions of the people around us.

Our parents, or initial guardians, help form our first set of beliefs because they are the ones who talk to us the most. We begin to apply the beliefs of our parents to new concepts and ideas that we haven't experienced yet. If our parents talk about how money is the root of all evil, we will believe it to be true because it's our first experience with money—even if it's only talked about. Although we may have never even seen how money has caused any evil, we accept the idea as true because we haven't learned anything different. Once we enter the world outside of our family tribe, our beliefs become confirmed or altered by our peers. We then begin to challenge the beliefs of our parents or accept them as being true. As we grow older, our beliefs become increasingly fixed, and we seldom seem willing to change them.

The problem is this: do the beliefs you hold right now really represent who you truly are? Do you think the real you actually has any doubts about what you can achieve? Do you think who you truly are hates anything about you?

We are all born wired to love, especially ourselves, and later we learn to hate. Hate is taught, love is natural.

> *"If people can learn to hate, they can be taught to love, for love comes more naturally to the human heart than its opposite."*
>
> – Nelson Mandela, Former President of South Africa

Your beliefs define who you are. But the beautiful thing about them is that they are all completely changeable, because beliefs are actually choices. The trick is to align your operating beliefs with the beliefs of your true self. But just because they are choices doesn't mean that beliefs are easy to change. Some can change very easily, but others are deeply rooted within us and will need extra work to turn around. But you can make the choice to put in that work, to choose to align your beliefs with who you truly are. That's why finding yourself is actually returning to yourself, returning to the true you who has nothing but love for who you really are.

One of my hideous masks used to be "Lazy Jamie." Growing

up, I really was one of the laziest people on Earth. Gaining my parents' approval depended on getting straight A's. As long as I got straight A's and respected other people, I made my parents proud. And if I didn't get straight A's, I was in big trouble—mainly because it meant I didn't try hard enough.

Getting their approval was very easy. I got straight A's without really doing any work at all. Memorizing and regurgitating useless information came naturally to me, and I was rewarded for it by getting straight A's. But it also rewarded me for being extremely lazy. So, since I was able to be lazy and still get straight A's, being rewarded for laziness was a side-effect of my parents' approval.

I became so lazy that when my parents asked me to mow the grass or trim the bushes, I would ask, "Why? It's just going to grow back in a week or two, and then I'm going to have to do it again! What's the point?!" Or when my mom asked me to run the dog for ten minutes, I would argue for twenty minutes about why I didn't want to. I would actually do more work trying to get out of doing the work that I was asked to do.

Laziness had followed me to college and afterwards into my career. I did just enough to not get fired. I would come into the office twenty to thirty minutes late and usually leave an hour before I was supposed to.

I was even too lazy to leave my apartment when I wasn't at work. I had a fear of "wasting" my time off. Grocery shopping on my day off? Seriously? When you can get food delivered? Laziness was my habitual behavior, and it seemed like there was nothing that would ever change that.

As a typical millennial, I have always wanted to change the world and make an impact, leaving it better than when I arrived. For hours on end, I entertained the question of how to take part in a cause bigger than myself. One day I was pondering this question while in the car, when the song "Man In the Mirror" by

Michael Jackson came on the radio. It was as if his lyrics came out of the speakers and slapped me across the face. "If you want to make the world a better place, take a look at yourself and make the change!"

In that moment, it felt like Michael was singing directly to me. As soon as I heard those lyrics, I thought to myself, "What is it that I need to change?" As I looked at myself in the rear view mirror, the answer hit me harder than the actual lyrics did: laziness. It's simply not possible to achieve anything worthwhile in this world with laziness as the baseline behavior. If I wanted to help make the world a better place, I had to learn how to work harder, smarter, and longer. And in order to change any behavior, we first have to change the belief we hold that causes that behavior.

Our belief system not only defines us, it also dictates our behavior. If we believe ourselves to be a lazy person, we will show the world how lazy we are. We will probably procrastinate, look for shortcuts and hope for those "get rich quick" schemes. If we believe we are an ugly person, we will behave like an ugly person. We may wear too much makeup if we are a girl, be shy around women if we are a guy, or we might be insecure about our appearance and reject any compliments that come our way. If we believe ourselves to be stupid, we will act like a stupid person. We will stop trying to learn anything new, let other people do everything for us, and think that all we know is all we ever will. Our beliefs show up in our habitual actions and behaviors. In the words of Tony Robbins, "Human Beings absolutely follow through with who they believe they are."

Beliefs are basically choices. You have a choice about what your beliefs are. The question is, do your current beliefs represent who you truly are? Do your current beliefs make you live and act in a way that makes you happy?

The greatest indication of whether or not our beliefs align

with our true selves is whether those beliefs allow us to love ourselves. My laziness didn't make me love myself. In fact, it made me hate myself because I innately knew that fulfillment and self-worth come from patience and effort. Laziness wants everything immediately and with the least amount of work. So the false belief that I am a "lazy" person had to change in order for my true self to shine. I didn't realize that I believed I was lazy until I tried to start working hard. I would start to work hard and then give up, thinking, "I'm just too lazy for this."

So I shifted my belief from "I am a lazy person" to "I was lazy at things I do not like." I didn't like to learn the subjects school forced on us. I didn't like to do yard work. I didn't like to work at that particular job. But I am actually a hard worker at things I am passionate about. So in order to work hard, I should always tie the passion I have for helping others into the work I do. This simple shift in my beliefs now has me working harder than I ever have before. And it doesn't feel like hard work anymore; instead, it gives me a feeling of passionate fulfillment.

To illustrate the idea that we live to be who we believe we are, Tony Robbins tells a story about a circus elephant. A circus elephant usually has a rope tied around its neck attached to a small stake in the ground. It could easily rip out the stake and set itself free if it wanted to, but it doesn't. Why? Because when it was a baby elephant, its trainers tied a rope around its neck and attached it to a very large stake in the ground. As hard as the baby elephant tried, it could never pull out the stake to get free. Eventually, it made the decision to believe, "It's not possible for me to pull this out." After the elephant made that decision, it never tried to pull out the stake again, even though it grew up to be strong enough to do so. The same can be said for you and me.

The people in our environments told us who we could and couldn't be when we were "baby elephants." People — usually teachers, parents, siblings or peers—tricked us into believing that we couldn't do certain things, that we aren't as attractive as society says we should be, and that our happiness comes from and relies on the outside world. In reality, the truth is that we can do anything we set our minds to. We are all as attractive as we believe *ourselves* to be, and our happiness relies on loving ourselves. But if we hold onto our false beliefs, we'll have nothing but doubts, self-hatred and the constant need for other people's approval. Beliefs are choices, so what beliefs would you now like to choose?

Remember Roger Bannister from earlier in this chapter? He broke the four-minute mile not only because he had the ability to do it, but because he had the belief that he could. When he first made up his mind and believed he could do it, he couldn't right away. He only had the belief. But his belief was so strong that he worked at it every single day. He trained and trained and trained until he had the skills and ability to run a four-minute mile. In a world where people believed that the four-minute mile was impossible, Roger Bannister *chose* to believe that it was possible. And you know what's interesting? After he did it, another person did it. Then another and another, and now more than 1,400 people have broken the four-minute mile. A feat that was once thought to be impossible has now been achieved by hundreds of people, and only because they believed it was possible, and they decided to train for it.

Henry Ford once said, "If you think you can do a thing or you think you can't do a thing, you're right." When we believe we can't do something, we don't even try. Why try if we don't think our effort will lead to success? We only put in the effort to go after the things we believe that we can achieve or have.

Think about how a child learns how to swim. You'll notice that as the child holds onto the edge of the pool, they are encouraged to swim over to the other side. When the child first lets go of the side, fear sets in and gets in the way, and the child continues to hold onto the side of the pool. Soon enough, beginner swimmers let go a little more each time, but they eventually come back to the edge of the pool. Then, all of a sudden, they let go completely, try their absolute best, and swim to the other side of the pool.

What happened? Did their skills change? Did they learn how to swim to the end of the pool all of sudden? No, they were always able to do it. What changed was the fact that they believed they could. The beliefs that we have dictate how we act in life. They dictate what effort we put into things, but they also dictate what we see in life.

When a robot observes its environment, it doesn't have a belief system, so it can't make judgments or come to conclusions about how things should be or look. Robots just see things as they are. In contrast, us humans either assign new beliefs to new experiences, or we see things from the context of our old set of beliefs.

The brain has what is called the Reticular Activating System. The job of this wonderful system is to filter out the information that we see on a moment-to-moment basis. Why? Because, through our five senses, our brain can receive almost eleven million bits of information per second. This special system filters the information taken in every moment. And what is the criterion your brain uses to filter what you see? Exactly what you believe about the world and yourself.

If we believe ourselves to be unattractive, our brain will filter information so we look unattractive. We could be the sexiest person alive, but if we don't believe it, then the mirror won't show it. We won't see all of the beauty that we are; we'll only see the pimple on the top of our forehead. If we believe ourselves to be stupid, our brain will look for reasons to confirm our stupidity. We could do a hundred different things a day in a very intelligent way, but our brain will only notice the one or two mistakes we made that make us feel stupid. When we believe something, our brain looks for an experience to confirm that belief, it finds one, and then that belief gets cemented into our very being—until we decide to change it. Both with ourselves and other people, we can only see things in the context of our belief system.

What are your beliefs? Do they make you love yourself? Do they align with who you truly are? With every belief that you have—about politics, religion, your view of yourself, your view of the world, the right way to treat others and yourself, etc. — ask yourself, "Does this belief allow me to love myself? If I hadn't been raised with this belief, would it still be mine?"

Change your beliefs, change your life. If you don't believe you can change, but you have the desire to change, all you lack is the belief in yourself. So your first step is to cultivate that belief. I've said it before, but I promise you: if I can change, anyone can. It just takes patience and effort, which are both skills you will learn about in this book. The time's going to go by anyway, so why not start now?

CHAPTER FOUR

The Lessons of Life

"The only real mistake is the one from which we learn nothing."

– Henry Ford, Business Magnate

Changing our beliefs to reflect who we truly are starts with knowing who we are not. The best way to learn who we are not is through the lessons of life — in other words, through the mistakes we have made and the challenges we have come across. There is a lesson in everything. We just have to look for it.

If you had known me in the past, especially when I was in the fraternity, you might have thought of me as a detriment to society. I have come a long way, but if it weren't for the lessons that life has taught me, I would not be where I am today.

Everything that happens to us is here to teach us a lesson. If we do something right, we learn to keep doing it. If we do something wrong, hopefully we learn to stop doing it. If we don't learn the lesson the first time, there is always an opportunity to learn it the next time, because if we keep making the same mistakes, the same consequences will arise. The cycle will repeat itself until we have learned the lesson and stop making the same mistakes.

A lot of my lessons thus far have been alcohol-related. I didn't start drinking until I was seventeen years old, and of course that night ended by me puking all over my friend's bathroom. You would think that would have stopped me then and there, but it didn't. The drinking carried on into college, where the parties got wilder.

In college I would constantly black out when I drank, never remembering anything from the night before. I could never figure out when it was time to stop, especially when I was drinking liquor. One moment I'd be having a grand ole time playing beer pong, and the next moment—really just the next morning—I'd wake up hungover (or still drunk), confused as to where I was. I made several stupid decisions while I was black-out drunk, which led me to wake up with many regrets. Yet, I never learned my lesson. I continued to drink liquor and black out when I drank too much.

In my junior year of college, I met a wonderful girl who helped me to begin turning my life around. I eventually started drinking less, and I slowly began dialing down my partying. Occasionally, however, I would still revert to a night out, drinking liquor and blacking out. It caused a lot of arguments between us, but I never learned the lesson.

Three years later, we were engaged. We didn't set a date, but we decided we probably would elope someday. One Labor Day weekend, we went to Las Vegas for a fun getaway. My friend went with us, but he stayed at a different hotel. When we arrived, we decided it was a great idea to elope that weekend. So we set the wedding venue, got our marriage license, and were ready to tie the knot. The day before the wedding, things turned the corner.

We were at the pool, and I thought it was a good idea to start the morning off with some margaritas. So I ordered a sixty-four-ounce margarita. Then another one. Then another one. But it didn't stop there; after all, it was Vegas, and I had a tequila sweet tooth! So I ordered a shot. Then another one. Then another one. Eventually, I was no longer Jamie.

I woke up in the middle of the night in my hotel room, next to a pile of puke on the bed. My then fiancée was nowhere to be found. This was one of the scariest moments of my life. I had no idea where she was or what had happened. I called her but got no answer. I called my friend; no answer. I went down to the casino to look for her—nothing. I went back to the hotel room and sat, waiting anxiously, until my friend called me the next morning.

He brought me coffee and then told me what had happened. I had been out of control with rage, throwing things around and being cruel to the one person who had always been there for me. It got to the point where she got scared and called my friend, asking to stay in his hotel room for the night.

I was beside myself with remorse. It didn't make any sense because it wasn't who I was or how I have ever acted. I immediately started bawling, feeling an intense amount of pain and regret. When I did see her that morning, my tears wouldn't stop. She forgave me soon after, but only because she could see the pain in my eyes. I had never cried in front of her before, and she knew how I acted the previous day was not who I am. We didn't get married then, and we eventually broke off our engagement a year later.

After we got back from the trip, I started seeing a therapist to try to understand what had happened. I decided to stop drinking for six months to clear my mind. When I began to drink again, I vowed to never black out ever again. I completely stopped drinking liquor, and haven't had a sip of it since that day.

The lesson of drinking in moderation had taken me a very long time to learn. I thankfully have finally learned it, and I am now such a better person for it. If we do not learn our lesson the first time, it will keep coming back — sometimes with worse consequences each time. Along with this horrible experience in Vegas came another lesson for me to learn: forgiveness. Although my then fiancée had forgiven me, I had not forgiven myself. Every time I thought back to that day, the feeling of guilt and shame came up again and again.

It wasn't until I heard the best definition of forgiveness I have ever heard that I was able to start forgiving myself: Forgiveness is a change in perception that removes a block in me, to my awareness of love's presence.

It's been said that man has only two real enemies: guilt and resentment. When we feel resentful or guilty about something, our energy is focused on hate. That hatred creates a block to the presence of love that surrounds us. To forgive means to remove that block, and it creates freed energy for more love for ourselves and other people—not just the people we have forgiven, but the other people around us too.

Forgiveness comes from the understanding that mistakes happen to teach us lessons. In order to change and progress through life, we must learn from our mistakes. But if we don't make mistakes in the first place, how will we ever learn?

We can either learn to forgive ourselves with the understanding that our mistakes make us better people, or we can continue to hate ourselves for something we cannot change. We cannot attain true, consistent happiness when we hate ourselves for things we have done in the past. In order to be consistently happy, we have to be able to learn to forgive ourselves. Everyone makes mistakes, but it's what we learn from our mistakes that determines whether our lives improve or not. To improve our lives, we have to learn the lessons that life is here to teach us. And if we wouldn't do the same thing again with the knowledge we have now, then guilt and shame cause us to convict an innocent person—a person who has learned from their mistakes and has used those lessons to improve their life.

Lessons come through our mistakes, but they also come from the negative situations, circumstances and experiences we encounter. Success is born out of the problems that we have. Those problems can either weigh us down, or they can be opportunities for us to soar.

Behind every experience, whether positive or negative, is the opportunity to learn something new. If we don't have the mindset of looking for the lesson, we brush bad experiences off as things that "just happen." If we look at negative events and circumstances as things that just happen to us, we miss the opportunity to grow.

When something happens, start asking yourself, "What's the lesson here? What can I learn from this?" This shift in perception from "woe is me; things just happen" to "I'm going to learn something from this" gives meaning to every experience in your life. Then there is a reason for the experience. You can learn how to prevent a similar experience from happening and also learn how to create a more positive one for you to enjoy in the future.

There is a lesson in everything, but the lesson isn't always obvious. If you can't figure out the lesson, decide on one yourself! As long as it moves your life in a positive direction, does it really matter what lesson you learn? If you were meant to learn a different lesson, then something similar will occur, and you'll have an opportunity to learn the lesson you were meant to next time around.

Sometimes things happen to us that are out of our control. We can take the approach of being a victim and complain about it to everyone who will listen. Or we can take the approach of being a captain who steers life in the direction we want it to go by learning from what life has given us.

About a year ago, I was talking on Tinder to a girl who happened to be in a wheelchair. She told me she had been in a car accident that left her paralyzed from the waist down. I asked her if she had learned anything from the experience. She said, "Yes, of course! It taught me gratitude, compassion, patience, and self-love."

Some people wouldn't have learned the same things from that car accident. They would have focused on being the victim instead of being the captain. Now she can use gratitude to be thankful for all of the little things that most of us take for granted. Now she can use compassion and patience when things aren't going the way she wants them to. Now she can use self-love to love others.

As we continued our conversation, I asked her, "So the accident taught you some important life lessons?" She then replied, "Yes, but who's to say I wouldn't have learned those lessons without the accident?" She very well might have, but the question is how long would it take for her to learn them some other way? The point here is speed. She wouldn't have learned those lessons in the time frame she had if it hadn't been for the accident. She matured twenty years faster without even realizing it.

We all go through things that seem to be unfair or out of our control, but it's not the event that defines us. The event helps make us. Ultimately, it's the lesson we choose to learn, the belief that comes along with the event, that defines us. We can choose to learn something from it that will improve our lives, or we can play the victim. The choice is always ours.

Learning from our mistakes and our experiences is only a piece of the puzzle, but it's an important one. Because after all, we might not know who we are if we haven't experienced who we are not. So when the lessons of life come knocking at your door, welcome them in and celebrate their arrival. When you celebrate the lessons you learn, you change your emotions from guilt and shame to love and happiness—love and happiness for the person you are becoming, instead of for the mask you used to wear.

Masks we wear are just lessons for us—to learn who we are not. But even when we know who we are not, it's easy to fall into that cycle of conditional happiness and approval, especially when we are so used to acting a certain way in front of certain people. Or even when we are in a situation where we meet new people, and their approval hangs in the balance. But it's important to remember to always be yourself. Because after all, happiness is the art of being yourself.

CHAPTER FIVE

The Art of Being Yourself

"The only way you're going to get through life, happily, is being yourself."

– Nikki Blonsky, Actress

What is happiness? If you google the definition of happiness, the answer comes up as "the state of being happy." Thanks, Google. Can you even define happiness? What happiness may look like to me may not be what happiness looks like to you. So how can we put happiness into words that apply to everyone?

When I quit my desk job to focus on myself, I took a serving job for temporary income. I knew it wasn't forever, so I tried to make the most of it while I was there. I noticed immediately how the other servers would get irritated at the smallest of things. "Can you believe they asked me for a refill? I'm not their server!" "Did you see my table brought an outside drink with them?" "Yep, happened again! My table ordered all waters!" Restaurants rank servers based on how many beverages they sell, which is why servers complain about people's drinks. Even so, these complaints sounded ridiculous to me. Another thing I noticed was how stressed everyone got when someone made a mistake.

After working at my desk job, serving seemed like a piece of cake. I didn't really complain about anything except for all of the people around me that were complaining. And stress? It was nonexistent. If I made a mistake at my past job, it could have cost someone millions of dollars. If I made a mistake as a server, it would only cost them a cheeseburger.

I wasn't excited to go to work every day, but I wasn't dreading it either. Actually, when I was at work serving, I noticed how happy I was. I couldn't figure out why I was so happy until it dawned on me: I was being completely myself without caring what anyone else thought about me. I knew there would be a time when I never see my co-workers again, so I never cared about their opinion of me.

I would dance foolishly in the kitchen. I would skip—yes, skip—in the hallways of the dining area. I would write positive notes on napkin-rolled silverware knowing no one would really care to read them. I did anything that came to mind without worrying how people would judge me. The happiness that came with that cannot be put into words. So we may not be able to define happiness, but we can define how to create happiness: The Art of Being Yourself.

Art is the expression of human creativity. In order to be your true self, you must first create your true self. You have the power to choose who you are, and in so choosing, you are creating yourself. Why? Because who you are is the accumulation of all your beliefs, and all beliefs are choices you make—to continue believing in them or to change them to represent who you truly are. So then, being yourself is actually an art form.

The thing to remember about choosing who you are is that you have a choice. This sounds obvious, but you'd be surprised how many people forget they can actually choose what they think, what they say, what they do, who they hang out with, and so on. Your capacity to choose is endless. You choose everything in your life, whether you do it consciously or not.

Unless you are incarcerated or held captive against your will, you always have a choice. The question is, what are you choosing? Are you choosing to make other people happy? Or are you choosing to make *you* happy?

Happiness comes from a feeling of love, but if we aren't being ourselves, then who is it that people are loving? So, we can look for the approval of others — consequently having people love someone who isn't real — or we can learn to love and approve of ourselves. With the former, our happiness depends on other people; in other words, our happiness is not within our control. With the latter, we gain control of our happiness, meaning our happiness becomes habitual. This doesn't mean we won't ever get sad or angry, it just means these emotions won't be our habitual state. Happiness will be.

In order to be ourselves, we must have and act on the beliefs that represent who we truly are. I have come up with three areas of my life that I believe dictate my levels of happiness. In other words, three areas of my life that allow me to express who I truly am:

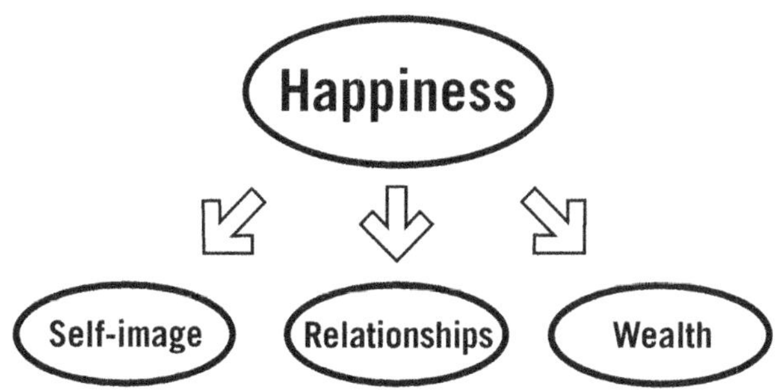

Your self-image is what you believe about yourself. If you don't see yourself as the true beauty that you are, how can you be happy? So let's start to shed the false negative beliefs you have about yourself and start to cultivate the self-love within you, because your true self loves everything about you.

Another area of life that allows you to be yourself is the people you spend time with. Harvard University conducted a seventy-five-year research study on happiness. The Harvard Study of Adult Development tracked the lives of seven hundred and twenty-four men. Harvard made two groups of people and periodically asked them questions about their lives, about home life, career and health. One group started as sophomores at Harvard college during World War Two. The other group was a group of young boys from Boston's most disadvantaged families of the 1930's. The results of the study were very interesting. Some climbed the social ladder from the bottom to the very top, and some went in the opposite direction. But the true takeaway was this: in both groups, it wasn't money or fame that resulted in the happiest and healthiest lives. It was the people's relationships that kept them happy and healthy. It's not the number of relationships you have, it's the quality of those relationships. It's about having true friends. True friends always encourage you to be yourself; fake friends encourage you to be like them. Real friends encourage you to make an impact; fake friends encourage you to only make money.

There has always been an assumption that money buys happiness. As the old saying goes, "Money may not buy happiness, but I'd rather cry in a Ferrari than in a Toyota." But as Gary Vaynerchuk always says, "I'd rather smile in a Toyota than cry in a Ferrari."

There are two ways you can define wealth. Most people's definition of wealth is the amount of money, fame, and "stuff" you have. My definition of wealth is the amount of impact you have on the world. The more money you have, the bigger the impact. Money isn't the goal, it's the byproduct of serving a cause greater than yourself. It's a byproduct of serving a cause that represents who you truly are and what makes you happy.

We will dive deeper into the diagram in later chapters. But as we go through each of these categories, think about what it is that you want in each of these areas. Where are you now, and where do you want to be?

The key word is "want" to be, not where you "think" you can be. Every great leader who has accomplished anything has told us that we all have the ability to achieve anything we set our minds to. The question is, what are you setting your mind to? What is the story that you believe about yourself?

The only thing that can stop us from achieving what we want in life is a false belief we have about ourselves. To quote Henry Ford again, "If you think you can do a thing or think you can't do a thing, you're right."

And as I said before, your belief system is entirely changeable. You have the ability to cultivate the belief in yourself with nothing more than patience and effort, so don't let your inner critic (which is really just other people inside your head) talk you out of going after what you really want in life. This is your life! Don't live it for other people. If you were to walk into most retirement homes, you would find the looks on most of the residents' faces frightening — the faces of unhappiness and regret. They aren't regretting that they didn't spend more time at work or wanting to have accumulated more money. The number one regret of the dying is that they wished they had had the courage to go after what they wanted in life instead of being afraid of other people's opinions.

If you want to live life in a state of habitual happiness and peaceful bliss, it is critical to focus on the approval of yourself rather than the approval of other people. In every situation, ask yourself, am I doing this because it represents who I am, or am I doing this because I want other people to like me? This isn't to say you should always be selfish. If you identify yourself as someone who helps others, then help others! Just don't help others at the expense of your self-worth, your self-image or the violation of your beliefs.

Also remember that constantly doing things for other people who take advantage of you is not helping them at all! If they keep taking advantage of you and you keep letting them, you're teaching them it's okay to take advantage of people. So if you really want to help them, tell them to p*ss off! You can do that more nicely than I would, but help them learn that it's not okay to manipulate people. They have the ability to do it on their own, even if they don't think they can or even want to. They may not see it as you helping them, but that doesn't really matter. All that matters is that you see that you're helping them, that you stay in line with who you are.

In the references section of this book, there are links to resources, what I call "fun-sheets," and other materials to help you with various things we talk about here. Shaking the need for the approval of others is one of them. You are never alone in this world unless you choose to be. Let this book, and the resources in it, help guide you to the habitual state of happiness.

This book can be your friend. And, as a friend, I encourage you to create yourself and then be yourself. The categories of the happiness diagram are the areas in my life in which I can represent who I truly am, and in turn, dictate my levels of happiness. There may be some areas in which you feel confident about being yourself and other areas in which you might not. But remember, this is my happiness diagram. After reading through each chapter, you may feel that some of the categories do not have anything to do with being who you are. You can adopt my happiness diagram, or you can make your own. Your happiness diagram may look something like this:

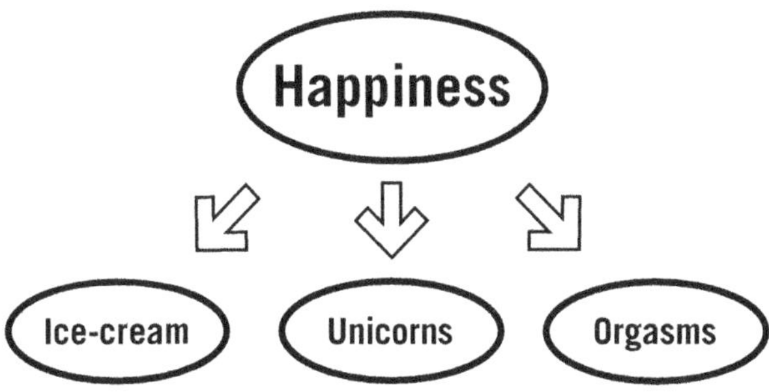

I don't judge. As long as you are happily being yourself, that's all that really matters.

CHAPTER SIX

The Mirror of Love

"To fall in love with yourself is the first secret to happiness."

- Robert Morley, Actor

When you look in the mirror, what do you see? What do you think of yourself when you are by yourself? If they aren't positive, self-loving thoughts, then I suggest it's time to rip off the mask.

It's not easy to know — or even acknowledge — that you have been wearing a mask. But if you have any thoughts about yourself that aren't positive and loving, I would recommend considering that you might be. Any thoughts — or, rather, beliefs — that you have about your appearance, your capabilities, or your worthiness that stir up anger, frustration, or an insecurity are part of a mask. Most of the time, these masks are created from other people putting their anger, frustrations, and insecurities onto us, after which we believed them to be true. But other times we are the ones who create the mask, leaving us to feel like we are living a life we are not meant to live.

Creating a mask, without consciously knowing we were doing it, was innocent at first. It was just to help us "fit in." It was there to help us feel like we were a part of something: a family, a community, or maybe a friendship circle. But wearing these masks leaves us confused. These masks make us believe that we are something we are not. They're a part of the voice inside our head that lies to us, that might tell us that we can't do it, that we're not attractive, or that we're not worthy enough.

Your true self loves everything about you. The true you is perfect in every way—including your imperfections. Your true self understands that we are all here to grow, and that as we age, we improve through our experiences, failures and successes. Your true self doesn't tell you that you can't do it; it knows that you can. Your true self doesn't tell you that you aren't good-looking; it knows that you are. Your true self doesn't tell you that you are worthless; it knows that your worth is beyond measure.

What we believe about ourselves is our self-image. Is your self-image a mirror of love or a mirror of the insecurities of other people? Which mirror do you want to use?

Unfortunately, our self-image is first created by other people when we were younger. As we grow older and our beliefs start to change, we either change that image or we keep it the same. Nonetheless, our self-image is first made through the tea that we drink.

What happens if your worst enemy pours a bucket of sugar in your tea, and you drink it? Then you've got really sweet tea. What happens if your best friend puts the tiniest drop of deadly poison in your tea, and you drink it? Then you're dead. The tea in this metaphor is like your mind. When you let someone, even your best friend, make you believe anything negative about yourself, you are drinking poisonous tea. This particular tea may not kill you, but it will kill the true self you were meant to be. It will shatter that mirror of love, the mirror of who you truly are.

If you are someone who does not love yourself exactly the way you are, you have drunk poisonous tea. That said, there is a difference between loving yourself and wanting more. It is human nature to want more, so you can love yourself and still want to get better. There's always room for improvement. But habitual happiness comes first from approving and loving yourself.

So how can we start to build that mirror of love? Loving and approving of ourselves starts with our health. Poor health, whether being overweight or always fatigued, is a clear indication that we aren't approving of ourselves—not because we have to be thin or look good to approve of ourselves—but because if we did approve of ourselves, we would treat our body with the respect it deserves. When we hate something about ourselves, we neglect ourselves. When we love ourselves fully, we respect ourselves and our body.

Your body absolutely loves you. It runs twenty-four hours a day, seven days a week to keep you alive and kicking. All it wants in return is to be moved, well nourished, and rested regularly. That's it. Nothing too fancy. But when you neglect these three things, your body isn't very happy, and when your body isn't happy, you aren't happy.

Being healthy in itself has its own benefits. When you're healthy, you feel good physically. You have the energy to do the things that represent you. If you're always tired, how are you going be enthusiastic about all the beautiful things you get to do with your life? Being healthy is great for energy, but it's even more important for confidence.

I have gone from being overweight in high school, to being skinny in college, to being almost obese in the world of work, to being muscular now. The difference being healthy has made in my self-confidence is night and day. When I was first overweight,

I was constantly self-conscious about my body. I had trouble talking to people of the opposite sex, was very shy in front of new people, and bullied others if I thought they would make fun of me. Then, when I lost forty pounds the first time, my personality shifted. I was able to be the true extrovert that I am and display a new sense of confidence that I didn't know existed.

Then I gained eighty pounds sitting at a desk all day. My confidence went from one hundred to zero. I was scared to speak up in meetings, thinking that my opinions didn't really matter. I isolated myself at home with my then fiancée, having found that it was easier to be comfortable there than to be around other people. I shifted my personality completely, from being outgoing to back to being shy, all because I was letting my weight define me. I wasn't allowing myself to be who I am.

So when I made the decision to feel that confidence again, it was because I knew what confidence had felt like in the past, and I desperately wanted it back. If you have always struggled with your weight — or even have insecurities and self-doubts — it may be hard for you to know the confidence I am describing. The feeling of being confident in your own skin is something I wouldn't trade for anything. There isn't enough money in the world to buy my confidence from me. It's that powerful.

I don't say this to induce shame or make anyone feel bad about themselves. I say this to inspire people who aren't confident to go for it. It is attainable! Even if you aren't overweight and do not feel confident, I promise you it is still attainable.

If you are truly confident—not cocky, but actually confident — and you're still overweight and happy, then by all means keep doing you! But if you're not confident, or you're just cocky (cocky meaning having a false sense of confidence that everyone can see right through), I highly encourage you to go after the way you want to look and feel.

It gives you this sense of accomplishment, this feeling that you put in the effort to better yourself, and that you have what it takes to accomplish new challenges. If you have tried in the past and haven't gotten very far, don't give up! I promise you that you can do it. It's all about adopting a strategy that's right for you. (If you want to learn more tips and strategies to help with exercising, nutrition, and confidence, please look at the "Skills to Learn" resource in the back after you have finished reading this book).

The next key area to help build that mirror of love is your diet. I'm not talking about diet as in the food you eat; I'm talking about your mental diet. Your mental diet consists of what you read (news/books/articles/social media posts, etc.), what you watch, the music you listen to, and the people you listen to. It's everything you feed into your mind. Your mental diet determines the way you open and close your mind to new ideas, the types of tea you do or do not drink.

The definition of an open mind is the ability to think about an idea without immediately rejecting it as false. It doesn't mean that you have to accept it as true; it just means you gave the idea a chance before you say it is false. After thinking about the idea, you may conclude that it doesn't align with your beliefs, but at least you gave it a chance. A closed mind rejects the new idea immediately and then proceeds to tell others "how it is." With certain ideas, we all have open and closed minds. The key to building a mirror of love is to strategize what you open and close your mind to.

What do you feed into your mind? Does your social media feed make you feel happy and uplifted? Or does it make you feel jealous and depressed? Your brain is always watching, and the more you feed it negativity, the more your Reticular Activating System looks for it.

I am completely out of touch with all of the gossip and negative news that surrounds the world. When people ask me, "Did you hear about what happened to Mrs. Jones down the street? Did you hear about what the president said? Did you hear about what so-and-so wore to the Oscars last night?" my response is usually, "Nope, not at all." I'd rather hear about a homeless man who helped return a child safely to their mother, or how a moving company bought a car for an employee who used to walk to work.

Sometimes people will ask me, "Well, how do you stay informed and aware of the bad things that are going on in the world?" Do I know that bad things happen in the world? Yes. But how much more aware do I have to be? Why should I focus on and talk to other people about the things I cannot control? All that does is bring a sense of fear and negativity into my life. I like being positive and happy. If there is a situation in which I can do something constructive or help in some way, then yes, I want to know about it. Otherwise, I'll feel helpless regarding the situation. So I do recommend sharing news of inspiration and positivity, and ignoring the rest. This can be kind of difficult because some people usually talk about the negative, but I'm telling you, the reward is worth the effort.

When the outside world is full of negative news, it can be hard to be positive. It's hard to keep that mirror of self-love if you're focused on what is wrong with the world. But as Tony Robbins says, the media isn't there to inform you, they're there to startle you so that you keep watching. So, keep your focus on what's right, especially in your world. Close your mind to ideas that counter the positive beliefs you have. Then keep your mind open to new ideas that have the potential to improve your life, regardless of whether they sound true or not. Do some research into it, or give it a try with an open mind. If you reject new ideas immediately just because they may sound "too good to be true," you may be preventing yourself from having a new belief that could dramatically improve your life. It only takes one new belief to change your life. Give yourself some time to process the new idea, then reject it if it still doesn't work for you.

The mirror of love is built by being selective with the information you take in, but it's also built through the information you put out. I'm talking about your dialogue, or the way you speak to yourself and to others. This also includes when you are in your head, thinking and talking to yourself.

How do you talk to yourself inside your head? How do you speak to yourself out loud? How do you talk about yourself to other people? Is it positive and uplifting? Or is it negative and depressing?

Eighty to ninety-five percent of all our thoughts today were the same thoughts as yesterday. How can we love ourselves if our dialogue (with ourselves and others) isn't loving? Our thoughts and words are choices we make. We either lift ourselves up or tear ourselves down. There are two main reasons we don't talk positively to ourselves:

1) Other people have tricked us into believing that what we do or who we are isn't good enough.

2) We don't think, talk or act in harmony with who we truly are.

If you've been tricked into believing you aren't good enough, it's probably because you've been trying to live someone else's life, or for someone else's approval. Of course you aren't good enough for what someone else wants! It's not the life you were meant to live! You are perfect for the life *you* want to live. You are perfect for who you really are. So start to build that mirror of love by deliberately shifting your dialogue.

If you constantly speak badly about yourself to yourself and to others, you will never love yourself. Your brain picks up on that. Your brain can't take a joke; it just believes what you tell it. Please remember that when you speak ill of yourself, even if you think it's just for a laugh.

Your self-dialogue isn't limited to the things you tell yourself; it also includes the questions you ask yourself. If you ask yourself a question that has an automatic negative answer, how do you think that will make you feel? If you ask yourself, "Why do I suck? Why am I so dumb? Why am I worthless?" your brain will always answer the question for you. When you ask yourself instead, "How can I get better? How can I improve? In what ways do I shine? What makes me worthy?" your brain will also answer those questions. When you start to ask yourself a negative question, immediately answer it with a positive affirmation: "Why do I suck? Wait a minute, I don't suck. I am learning, I am growing, and I am getting better with every mistake that I make!"

This is why affirmations are so powerful. An affirmation is a kind, positive statement that you affirm to yourself. You repeat the positive statement over and over until it becomes ingrained into your belief system. Usually affirmations are done while you are looking at yourself in the mirror.

Here are some examples: "I am worthy! I am love! I am strong! I can do anything I set my mind to!" The key to affirmations is to say them strongly, boldly, with enthusiasm and with positive emotion behind them. Choose your affirmations based on what belief you want to cultivate about yourself! Whether that's patience, kindness, love or excitement, choose what you would like to believe about yourself, what your true self already knows about you.

When you start to do affirmations, you may feel like they are pointless. You may even disagree with your statement, and start to tell yourself the opposite. It's important to keep doing them. Make it a daily habit that for five minutes in the morning and/or at night, you will affirm to yourself that you are awesome, or whatever it is that you want to believe. If you keep it up, that inner critic will start to go away. Each day you'll feel more and more confident that you are awesome, worthy, lovable, loving and strong—because you actually are. It's like going to the gym. When you first start out, it may seem like it's not accomplishing anything. But you see the results over time, not after one workout or one session of affirmations. So keep doing them to build that mirror of love.

Most of your dialogue, whether it's your thoughts about yourself or the way you speak to others, is habitual. This means you follow the same pattern of thinking and talking over and over, whether it's uplifting or degrading. Breaking a habit can be very difficult, unless you *replace* it with another habit.

Replacing a habit is quite simple. The first step is awareness. It's being aware that you're saying or doing the original behavior. So, if you tell yourself that you aren't pretty, or that you aren't good enough (or that you're worthless or fat, or any of the other negative things you might tell yourself or others), the first step is to catch yourself saying it. If you catch yourself in the middle of the behavior, or during a sentence, stop immediately. The next step is to instantly say the opposite of what you usually say, or the new belief that represents who you truly are.

Let's say that you have a preconceived notion that you aren't smart. Everyone is smart in their own way, and after reading this book, I hope you'll know this to be true. But the only way to actually believe it is to change your internal dialogue.

Let's say you make a mistake at work or miss a question on a test. At first you may think, "How could I mess that up? I'm so dumb." Again, for emphasis, the first step is to catch yourself doing or saying it. When you catch yourself, it's important not to judge yourself. Respond with compassion, with the understanding that you are learning. Change is a process, not an event. As Carl Jung used to say, what you resist persists, so judging yourself negates change. So with compassion, after catching yourself, say to yourself, "It's okay to make mistakes. It doesn't make me dumb. I am smart in my own way, and I will learn from this." If you do this enough times with patience and effort, you'll start to think and talk in a completely different way.

Physical health, mental diets, dialogue, affirmations and replacing habits are all ways to build that mirror of love. But the way to get started is with intentions. Be intentional with everything you do. Describe in detail who you are. Not who you are right now, or the mask you've been wearing, but the you that you know you can be. The you that you know you truly are.

What do you want to believe about yourself? Write it down. If you're unsure, start with the most negative belief you have about yourself, the one that is keeping you from loving yourself fully. Then write down what you want to believe about yourself in that regard, or simply the opposite of what you believe now.

Then start to be intentional with your thoughts, words, and actions. Constantly ask yourself, "Does this represent who I am, the true me I'm going to be? Are these words in harmony with who I am? Does this action represent me?" Ask these questions about everything: your job, your relationships, your mindset, your appearance, your health—everything. Write down the things you want to change and start to create the belief that you can change them by using your mental diets, dialogue, affirmations and new habits. Start with a couple at a time. Otherwise, you might get overwhelmed. This all will require discipline, which is a skill you will learn about in the resources sections.

The mirror of love is obviously about loving yourself, but more importantly, it's about switching from other people's approval to self-approval. The difference between the two explains *everything* that you do.

Do you work out so you look sexy to others? Or do you exercise so you feel sexy for *yourself*? Do you dress for the latest fashion trends, the things other people think are "in"? Or do you dress for what *you* think looks cool? Do you style your hair for others or for *yourself*? If you wear makeup, do you wear makeup so that others think you're pretty, or do you wear makeup so *you* think you're pretty?

The mirror of self-love isn't just about what's on the inside, it's also about what's on the outside. Your appearance tells the outside world who you are. Does your appearance tell people that you are searching for their approval, or does it say, "I approve of myself"? If you always dress to "fit in," you are not dressing for your own approval. People always say, "Dress to impress." Absolutely, dress to impress…yourself.

When we wear clothes that do not represent who we are, we immediately feel like an imposter. We feel as if we don't fit in, even though we are wearing exactly what everyone else is wearing, trying to fit in. It's hard to be yourself when you feel like an imposter, when you look like an imposter, and of course when you *are* an imposter.

If your employer has a mandatory dress code, find a way to make sure your outfits represent you anyway. There's always a style that you can align yourself with, even if it's business or business casual. Try different things out and see what feels like you and what doesn't.

Dress to impress yourself. Wear things not because you look good in them, but because you feel good in them. You can look good and feel good at the same time. Just don't sacrifice being yourself to look good for other people. Clothes were made to make us feel comfortable, not to divide the cool from the uncool. So be comfortable in your own shoes, literally.

Your self-image is vital to your happiness, to allowing yourself to be who you truly are. It's your first step to *creating* who you truly are. Once you've developed a positive self-image for yourself, a mirror of love, you have to protect it. Here are some tips on protecting your self-image:

1. Don't let anyone call you by the wrong name or mispronounce your name.

My name is Jamie Naegele, pronounced JAY-mee NAY-glee. If you mispronounce it or call me something else, I will politely correct you. Not in a pompous, "You should know how to say my name" way, but in a loving, "My name is important to me" way.

The words of your name are among the most important words ever spoken to you. When someone calls you by the wrong name or mispronounces it, it stings a little. It makes it seem as if they don't care. But if you don't help by politely correcting them, it makes it seem like *you* don't care. It doesn't matter if your name looks like Xsijdhfpiuashdfpius. Always correct anyone who says your name incorrectly, but please do it kindly. If you know your name is hard to pronounce or a name that's foreign to the country you're in, be patient with others. Most people want to get your name right, but if it's a name they aren't familiar with, it can be tricky. Understand that it may take time for them to get it right, but make sure that they eventually do get it right.

2. If you say you're going to do something, do it.

Your brain notices when you say you're going to do something and then back out of it. It then thinks you are a liar to yourself, and that makes it harder to believe different things about you. Are you going to stick one hundred percent to all of your commitments? Probably not, but at least make an effort to stick to your word as much as possible. Most people's commitments to themselves are meant to improve their lives, and I'm sure yours are too. The more you follow through on your positive commitments, the more your life will improve. You'll learn more about how to follow through with your commitments later in this book, but realize that it is important.

3. Practice healthy competition.

Some people say that money is the root of all evil. I wholeheartedly disagree. Money isn't the root of all evil: unhealthy competition is the root of all evil.

There is a major difference between healthy and unhealthy competition. Healthy competition inspires us to strive for more. It's the realization that, "Hey, he's doing better than me. What's he doing that I'm not? How can I learn from him? What can he teach me so that I do better?" Healthy competition encourages collaboration. When we are in healthy competition with one another, we realize that by helping each other, we can make each other stronger. We can make each other better. You are better at some things than I am, and vice versa. You know things that I do not, and vice versa. By sharing and trading information collaboratively, without holding anything back, we build each other up.

Unhealthy competition is the complete opposite. It's, "Hey, he's doing better than me! How can I tear him down? How can I take advantage of him so that I *feel* better? What can I do to flip the script?" Unhealthy competition causes businesses to focus on how to beat and ruin their competitors, instead of putting their time and energy into improving themselves. It makes politicians slander other candidates to make themselves look like a better choice. It causes football players to try to injure the other team's best players. It causes people to hoard money and information so that they stay on top, without ever realizing that they can get even better by sharing and giving. It's this mentality of having to win versus striving to get better that makes us forget our humanity. That line of thinking is the root of all evil.

It is caused by making negative comparisons with others. It can even make people stop learning skills they love. Instead of thinking, "How can I become as good as he is?" they think, "I'll never be as good as them." That makes them want to quit instead of being inspired to pursue the skills they love relentlessly.

When you view comparisons as a way to improve your life, you eliminate that negative aspect. Again, the toddler doesn't see others walking and think, "I can't walk." The toddler sees others walking and wonders, "How can I walk too?" When you think the way the toddler does, you view others as examples of "I can, too." This change in perception gives you a preview of what you, too, can accomplish. It gives you more tools in your tool belt to build your mirror of self-love. But make sure to use those tools, to apply them, so that you actually build it.

Build your self-image into the mirror of love that you deserve. Whatever that mirror looks like to you, build it with confidence. It's impossible not to change in a positive direction if you focus on it with patience and effort. The first step is deciding that you will. Build the mirror of love, and then protect it.

If you don't currently love every aspect of yourself, until now it's not your fault. Someone else tricked you into disliking aspects of yourself, and not knowing this has prevented you from changing. But now you know. Now you have the tools to start to build that mirror of love. If you decide not to use the tools, then it does become your fault. It may take time, but as I said before, the time will pass by anyway, so choose to use it wisely.

In the next chapter we will discuss relationships. You are responsible for building the mirror of love, but it's the people you spend time with that will help you maintain it—or destroy it.

CHAPTER SEVEN

OQP

"OQP — Only Quality People."

– Les Brown, Professional Speaker

What do your relationships mean to you? Your friends, your family, your possible lover(s)—what do they mean to you? Are they a source of joy, freedom and laugher? Or are they a source of misery, restrictions and frustration? Every relationship is different, but what's the overall feeling you get with the people you spend most of your time with? Do most of them lift you up and encourage you? Or are they the critics inside your head, telling you lies that make you hate something about yourself?

Every peer group I have ever been a part of has influenced my life in one way or another. In high school, my friends would constantly make fun of each other—as ruthlessly as possible. We prided ourselves on who could make our other friends laugh the most, usually at the expense of someone else. Everyone was made fun of, everyone made fun of others, and this helped create the mask of "The Bully."

When I worked at the desk job, I didn't have any friends outside of work. I was actually afraid to leave my apartment from a sense of comfort there and a lack of self-confidence elsewhere. So the people I hung around the most were my co-workers, who believed in the lifestyle of work hard, play hard — but work harder. There is nothing wrong with that lifestyle unless it makes you unhealthy, in physical or mental health and in relationships. I wanted people to think I worked hard, to think I was successful, but I became unhealthy in all of those areas. As a result, the mask called "Pretend-Success Jamie" was born.

Then there was the lazy version of myself. It wasn't so much the people I hung out with, but the people I *didn't* hang out with. I didn't have friends who inspired me to grow. I didn't have friends who encouraged me to go after what I wanted in life and to work to be the best version of myself that I could be. With no one around me to inspire me to be myself, the mask called "Lazy Jamie" came to life.

These masks were the result of the people I chose or didn't choose to hang around. However, just because I chose to "fit in" does not make the people from my past bad people. Most of them were actually phenomenal people; it was the friendships that I had helped create that were terrible. It was me who didn't inspire them to grow, who didn't encourage them to go after what they wanted in life, and who chose to wear those masks. And as I said earlier, it's always about treating others the way you want to be treated, because that's how they will treat you. It wasn't until I realized who were actually true friends and who were not that I was able to become selective about the people I chose to spend time with. The mask of "The Frat Star" helped teach me this lesson.

When I was in a fraternity in college, my friends and I always wanted to party. Six days a week spent drinking with one day for recovery was the norm. There were many times where some of us reached the point of "I just don't feel like drinking tonight" or "I think I've had enough to drink tonight." The immediate reaction from everyone was, "P*ssy! You're a P*ssy!" And then, of course, I or someone else would say, "Oh really? Pour me a shot. Oh yeah? Watch me shotgun this beer!" It was like all of our manhoods were dependent on how much we could drink.

When you're in a fraternity, it feels like it's a brotherhood. You all go through a lot together to be allowed into the fraternity, so I considered everyone in my fraternity not only my friend, but my actual brother as well.

Surprisingly, our fraternity eventually got into a lot of trouble that drew the attention of our national fraternity (not surprising at all). The national fraternity is the organization that is technically in charge of all of those particular fraternities at every college. They made a full investigation into us to determine if we would be kicked off campus.

Eventually they decided to kick some brothers out of the fraternity and keep some brothers in. I ended up getting formally removed from the fraternity — but everyone knows that once you're in, you're in for life — or so I thought. However, the national fraternity told the remaining brothers that if they allowed any of the kicked-out members back into the fraternity house, the whole fraternity would be kicked off campus.

The national fraternity had no way of knowing who came through the house because they were never there, but some of the remaining fraternity brothers viewed the threat as a very real possibility. So, whenever I showed up at the house, I was usually told to leave. A lot of the brothers didn't really care, but if the ones who did care got wind that I was there, they gathered as many brothers as they could to make sure I left immediately. When things got challenging, people showed their true colors. This was one of the lessons I had to learn, that not everyone I think is my friend is actually my friend.

This is a silly example of greek life drama, but it's where I first had to learn this lesson. Have you learned this lesson? Do you hang around people you think are your friends, but actually might not be? A true friend is someone I call a "quality" person. There are usually three types of people that we know: cancers, quality people and acquaintances.

Some people are what I call a "cancer." They're cancerous because they are the people who are there to kill your true self, your hopes and your dreams. Some might even call them "energy vampires" because they literally drain the life you were meant to live out of you. These are the people who complain about everyone and everything. They are the first to tell you that you are wrong and most likely give you false criticism. These people are the critics inside your head, telling you lies that cause you to hate a part of yourself. They tell you that you can't do something, that your dreams are unattainable. (When people tell you that you can't do something, it's really a reflection of what they can't see themselves doing). They're the ones you may be afraid to show your true self to because their judgments are always guaranteed.

A quality person, on the other hand, is someone who inspires you to grow. These people encourage you to move toward your dreams, never putting any doubt on you. They are people you can count on, no matter the situation. When you're in need, they are there to help you, no favors asked in return. And if they do ask, it's always in a joking fashion that really says, "You owe me, but I know you'd be there for me even if you didn't." A quality person is someone whom you can be your total self with, and will love you for being you without trying to change you. Quality people won't try to change the real you, but they will try to push you to be the person they know you want to be. Not who *they* want you to be, but who *you* want to be. They are not the people who tell you what you want to hear; they tell you what you *need* to hear. Being a quality person isn't just about being kind. Being kind is important, but it's also about being honest and pushing people to their fullest potential. A quality person is someone you would call your true friend.

An acquaintance is someone you hang out with sometimes, or even regularly. It's someone you might have fun with, but not someone you would rely on when things get difficult. Someone you know on the surface, but not someone you connect with on a deep level. It's someone who has the potential to be a real friend, but it also could be someone you wear a mask for. In other words, acquaintances could be quality people or cancers. You can't really be sure, because you don't know the real them well enough.

There is a simple way that you can determine who is a quality person and who is not. I call it the "friend test." If you have a goal that you are striving for — dieting, exercising, fasting, financial, etc. — do your friends encourage you to keep going or to quit if you ever feel like giving up? If you tell your friends that you're thinking about stopping, do they tell you to keep going and that you can do it? Or do they tell you that it is hard and they don't blame you for quitting? Or do they even *encourage* you to give up, telling you that you won't accomplish it anyway? A quality person will never encourage you to give up on your goals or your dreams — even if that conflicts with their own interests of spending more time with you. So, the answer to those questions might determine the type of person you are dealing with.

It's also a good point to note that just because someone is not a quality person now, doesn't mean they never will be. People can change, and you do have the ability to remind them of your goals—teaching them how to be a quality person along the way. But you can't change anyone. So if they are not willing to change, please do not even try.

It's been said that you are the average of the five people you spend the most time with. How many of the five people you hang around most are quality people? Is it all five? Three? One? Zero? Let me ask it in a different way. Are you yourself 100% a quality person? 60%? 20%? Not a quality person at all?

These questions are not meant to insult you, but to get you to think about the people you hang around. We all mirror the people we hang with in some way or another, whether it's in our lingo, behavior, or attitude. There's nothing wrong with that, unless the people we are mirroring aren't quality people.

I'm not just talking about your friends; I'm talking about your family members and your lover(s) too. I'm talking about all of your relationships. They all matter. You can choose your friends and lover(s), but you can't choose your family. You can, however, choose the amount of time you spend with your family and the boundaries you set with them.

Our families can be a great source of joy for us, but sometimes they can also be a source of pain and insecurities. If you have siblings, then you know the sibling dynamic can be full of emotions. I know that as an older brother growing up, I teased my younger brother constantly. I think at a very young age it was just because he was the new son, with whom I felt I had to compete for attention. But as we got older, it was mainly because I was jealous of him for being more athletic than me. So I made fun of him and bullied him a lot.

Teasing other people doesn't always seem like bullying because we assume that everyone knows that the teasing is just a joke. Even when we are with friends, we can still tease and laugh at each other. But if the other person doesn't know we are joking around, or we laugh at them for the same thing over and over, they may start to believe what we are saying is actually true.

I had a very good friend growing up whom I used to look up to. In my mind, he was probably one of the coolest dudes I knew at the time. He was funny, extremely good looking, muscular, friendly, and confident—but sometimes he would jokingly make fun of other people. Honestly, there wasn't really anything that anyone could tease or make fun of him for back, but they picked one anyway. Because he was a muscular guy, his neck was bigger than most people's. It wasn't humongous, but that didn't stop people from telling him it was.

Everyone made fun of him for having a huge neck. Whenever he got a little too confident in what he was saying, people would use that against him to bring him down a couple of notches. It was all just fun and games, teasing between friends.

One night, we were drinking together. I don't really remember everything that was said, but I'll never forget what happened. It had something to do with a girl, and I told him something along the lines of, "You'll be alright. You're a good looking dude." He was drunk, so his inhibitions were down, and he replied, "Yeah, but my neck is huge." It was something he seemed to be very insecure about. He didn't even have that big of a neck! When I told him that, he responded with, "Then why does everyone say that I do?"

What he didn't realize was that they didn't have anything else to tease him about, so they told him he had a huge neck — and he believed them. Teasing is fine when we all know we are just messing around. But when we are constantly getting teased for the same things, we start to believe them — even though they're probably not true.

At some points in our lives, we all deal with or interact with people who tease us. Many people even go so far as to think that those being teased are "wussies" if they can't take the heat. I view that mentality as just another mask, wanting some reason to feel better than another. I know because I used to be one of them.

If people start to tease you for things you cannot control, or they constantly call you stupid or dumb when you make little mistakes, you have to defend your mirror of love from them. It doesn't matter if it's your teenage sister or your thirty-year-old son, you have to shield your mirror of love.

One way you can do this is by telling them that you don't believe them, or that what they're saying isn't true. Not because you want them to believe it or because you need their approval, but because your mirror of love depends on *you* believing it. To do that, you must be able to do it nicely, confidently, and repeatedly, or else you might come across as defending yourself — to them and to you. When you believe in yourself, you don't need to defend it, because it's not conditional on whether other people believe in you too.

Jokes and teasing can be okay if everyone knows that's all it is, and if we aren't hammering each other for the same things over and over again (especially if it's something we can't control even if we wanted to). Just because someone teases us sometimes doesn't automatically make them a cancer or a non-quality person. It's just when that's their habitual behavior or they do it with malicious intent that they become a cancer. Sometimes, life requires us to be around people who are not quality people—whether through work or in communities, so "Only Quality People" (OQP) doesn't refer to spending time with quality people only — as counterintuitive as that sounds. It's about hanging around quality people most of the time, having OQP in your inner circle. It's about having at least the five people you hang around most be quality people. It's distinguishing between who is a true friend, who (for the moment) is an acquaintance, and who is a cancer. It's nourishing the relationships you have with quality people, determining the relationship you want to have with the acquaintances, and dealing with the cancers of your life.

There are three ways to deal with a "cancer." You can perform surgery and cut them out of your life completely. You can live with them and try as hard as you possibly can to contain their damage by limiting your exposure to them — which can be a good learning opportunity on how to be yourself in the face of their judgments and unhelpful criticisms. Or, you can continue to conform to what they want for you, and let the cancer destroy you, which I do not recommend. The more time you spend with cancers, the less time you can spend with quality friends and developing quality friendships.

Friendship is a skill. It takes patience and effort to develop a quality friendship or relationship with someone. A quality relationship, in any regard, comes from building a deep, meaningful connection with another.

I like to people-watch when I go to restaurants. Some people's interactions can be so entertaining. My people-watching skills used to be terrible. I would literally just stare at the other table, clearly eavesdropping on their conversations. My former fiancée would constantly criticize me for creeping in on other people's conversations. I finally figured out, years later when I started my "Lone Wolf" journey, that staring at people when you're eating alone is far creepier than doing it when you're with someone else (even though both are still pretty creepy).

I was at a small cafe one day, and I noticed two people who were clearly either on a first date or had just started dating. It seemed like they were having a great conversation and she was really into it. Then out of nowhere, he pulled out his phone and started mindlessly scrolling. She sat there quietly, visibly irked, when finally she caved and pulled out her phone, too. He tried to show her something funny on his phone, and she gave him the "cool, bro" fake smile. As they left the cafe, I realized how often I used to do that with the people around me. How can we build deep, meaningful connections with people if we value virtual people more than actual people? The answer is, we can't.

The truth is we don't even value virtual people more, we just value not being bored. The phone has replaced boredom. Before the changes technology has brought, people had to figure out ways to get rid of boredom. Children actually played outside! Now they have video games and an iPad to satisfy them. Backyard whiffle ball has turned into a staring contest between children and their screens. But even adults use their phones to relieve boredom. It's an easy way to entertain ourselves; just whip out your phone and scroll mindlessly. Three hours of TikTok and you've forgotten what time it is. The sad part is we even do this in front of other people! Why? Why are we so bored around other people? Because our conversations are so boring!

How can we form a deep, meaningful connection with someone without having deep, meaningful conversations? A lot of people are afraid to have deep, meaningful conversations with other people. These conversations require vulnerability. They require us to put our guard down, share our true feelings and opinions, and risk rejection.

Everyone wants to have deep, meaningful connections — they just don't want to risk the rejection. How can we form a deep connection with someone using shallow conversations? It's the classic get-rich-quick scheme, but with relationships. Some women only talk about other people, gossip and judgments, and some men only talk about sports and women, balls and boobs. In between is the dreaded small talk: what the weather's been like, and how little Johnny is enjoying summer camp.

One of the reasons people are afraid to have these deep conversations is because they've been hurt by previous rejections by people they cared about. So they have built these walls up to protect themselves from being hurt again, while consequently blocking other people from entering. But the walls do not just keep people out. They also keep problems and emotions trapped in. Most people only let their guard down when they get triggered by something or get drunk, and then their problems and true feelings come out like a tidal wave that has been bottled up for too long.

Building walls is a defense mechanism for protecting ourselves. This was probably because we allowed the wrong people into our lives in the first place, or the right people ended up walking away. But having true, quality relationships doesn't depend on allowing everyone into your life. It's about letting the people into your life who are worth the risk of you getting hurt — people who inspire you to grow, teach you to love yourself and make you feel special. Because the truth is, it wasn't they who made you feel special; they taught you how you can make yourself feel special. If they do part company with you, then it is time to take what they have taught you and apply it to yourself!

If they called you beautiful every morning, why don't you do the same? If they made you feel sexy about yourself, why don't you do the same? What did they do that made you feel that way? Then do it for yourself! Take what they have taught you about yourself, and turn it into the mirror of love!

Not everyone is meant to be in our lives forever, but everyone who has been in our lives was meant to teach us something forever — to take what they have taught us and to use it for the rest of our lives. Some people are meant to teach us patience, others compassion. It all depends on how you look at the relationship. Do you focus on what's missing, or on what you have gained? The choice is always yours.

You can only form deep, meaningful relationships with people by becoming vulnerable and showing your true, authentic self.

When relationships fail, it's usually because people are trying to force others to be something they are not. Relationships are meant to be instances of people, who are authentically being themselves, coming together to form a partnership or group (friends, family, or lovers) that love each other for who they really are. Who you are is always yours and is never tied to the people in your life. Should compromises be made in a relationship? Absolutely, but none that compromise the integrity of who you truly are, because happiness, in relationships and in life, comes from loving and being yourself. It doesn't come from conforming to please others — even if conforming would be the only way to maintain the relationship.

Happiness is contagious. People want to be around happy people because they get a sense of enthusiasm from happy people. They feel welcomed to be themselves in the presence of others who are being themselves. People who are themselves are usually the people who have deep, meaningful conversations because they don't care about the possibility of rejection. They don't need others' approval. They have their own approval.

So if you want to be yourself, find people who you can be yourself with. Find the quality people who won't judge you. Find people who lift you up, not tear you down. If you're constantly with people who tear you down, you'll start to believe their lies. And that's all they are: lies. As I hope you know now, your true self loves you. And anyone who doesn't love your true self, doesn't deserve to take away your contagious happiness.

The only thing as contagious as happiness is misery. Misery loves company and seeks to create company wherever it can. Happiness just loves happiness and seeks to create more happiness. Misery creates other miserable people. Happiness creates other happy people. It's that simple.

Build the mirror of love. Keep it with the people around you, and always remember: OQP – Only Quality People.

CHAPTER EIGHT

Skillz Pay the Billz

"The best investment you can make, is an investment in yourself. The more you learn the more you earn."

– Warren Buffet, Business Magnate

Your wealth plays a large part in your happiness. Your wealth is created by your skill set, your career and your investments (or sources of income other than your primary job). Each of these components represents an opportunity to help express who you are.

Without a certain amount of money, being happy can be very difficult. When you're constantly worried about where your next meal will come from, or how to keep your kids warm, or anything else that would cause you to worry about money, being happy can be nonexistent.

However, beyond a certain amount of it in the bank, money won't increase your happiness. A lot of people believe that it will, but ask anyone who is honest who has been down that road. We hear it often: "Money can't buy happiness." So why is it that we all continue to think that it will?

Sometimes it's because we believe that more money will lead us to more experiences — more vacations, new toys, etc. The truth is, more money will absolutely lead to more experiences. But more experiences, without loving ourselves first, will only lead us to experiencing more of life without the feeling of true love or habitual happiness. We'll visit all of the lavish destinations, dine at the finest of restaurants, and enjoy all the luxuries life has to offer, but with a feeling of emptiness inside — the feeling that something's missing. So we'll try to fill that void with more money and more experiences, but what is actually missing is what our hearts desire most: love.

Other times we think happiness can be bought because we think that happiness comes from the approval of others. If we just had more money or more fame, then we could become more popular — and more popularity means more approval. But if we don't love ourselves, what is the point of being popular? It will only lead us to chase more approval — that fake feeling that we are loved by others, when the love for ourselves is all that matters.

It also doesn't help that some people who have a lot of money *pretend* that they are happy — when they are really only searching for approval too. They post all their vacations, mansions, cars, and parties on social media. They smile in the picture, but frown in the mirror. Most people tend to think that happiness can be bought, so they'll go spend $1,000 to get the latest iPhone with all its new features and for the status it feels like it brings, because they think that will bring them happiness.

Think back to a time when you may have thought a new purchase would make you happy. It probably did, but only for a few days — leaving you to search for happiness in the next purchase. Things will only bring short-term, conditional happiness. So, instead of spending money on unnecessary purchases, you could be spending that money on learning money skills.

Earning, spending and keeping money are all skills. If you haven't learned these skills, someone can give you all the money in the world and you'll remain where you are now. It may take several years to get back to where you are, and you may have an enormous amount of "fun" along the way, but get back there you shall. You'll probably end up worse off than you are now, because your fun was taken away. Ask any lottery winner. They are three to four times more likely to go bankrupt than the average American. That's because they didn't spend time learning the skill set of earning, spending and keeping money. They don't teach us these skills in school, so we have to be able to learn them for ourselves.

If you do find yourself with an unexpected large sum of cash, please do yourself a favor and invest the time and money to learn money skills first. The key word here is to learn, not handle. If you hire someone to handle your money instead of learning the skills yourself, you will always be at the mercy of someone else's skill set. It's necessary to rely on other people's skill sets for help with some matters, but money is not one of them. I'm not saying to be reckless and to try and do it all yourself from the get go. It is important to get financial advice until you can learn how to manage money, but it's equally important to learn the skill set of handling money yourself. You don't have to have a lot of money or be mentored by someone to get started. We live in the age of information; all you need is a good book or the internet to be your teacher. Keep building on the skills you learn, and then start to invest in your skills—because the more you learn, the more you truly earn.

Everything is a skill. EVERYTHING IS A SKILL. Kindness is a skill. Patience is a skill. Forgiveness is a skill. Compassion, raising a child, cooking, exercise, math, creativity, trust, gratitude, memory, confidence, learning (and self-learning) and teaching are all skills we can learn. Happiness is a skill. Being yourself is a skill. Do you get the point? Everything is a skill.

A lot of people think that some people are just born with certain skills and others aren't, so they call those skills "talents." Talent means you are born with exceptionally high levels of a particular skill. However, that does not mean that if you aren't born with talent that you cannot learn and become exceptionally good at that skill too. Everyone can learn and improve at any skill, even if they do not have the talent. All you need is the belief that you can, the effort and discipline to put in the work, and the patience to get back up if or when you fail.

Think of all your skills as your wealth tool belt. The more you learn, the more you earn. So the more tools you have in your tool belt, the better the masterpiece you can create. In order to be able to have the wealth tool belt in the first place, you need to be able to create the actual belt and the compartments to hold all of your tools. The belt, which holds the compartments together, is the skill of cultivating the belief that you can learn new skills. The material that forms the compartments for your tools is the skill of effort. Without these two skills, you will never be able to learn anything new.

If you do not believe you can learn and get better at a particular skill, you will never put in the effort to try. Why bother if you don't think it's possible? Usually, there are certain skills you think you can learn and some you can't, so your tool belt will only be able to hold the skills you think you can learn. I promise you: you can learn any skill unless you tell yourself you can't. If you have studied mindsets before, you know that I'm talking about a growth mindset, which was discovered by Dr. Carol Dweck. Thank God for Carol.

There are two types of skills: physical skills and mental

skills. Physical skills are skills such as cooking, math, memory, tennis, golf, cleaning, etc. They are improved upon and developed through physical practice: failing, learning, succeeding, and repeat. With each failure and success, you learn something new about the skill that will help you improve. After each success you'll learn what to do; after each failure you'll learn what not to do.

Mental skills are skills like trust, patience, forgiveness, confidence and compassion. Mental skills are developed through mental practice, and the way you practice mental skills is the same way you practice mindfulness during meditation. There are many forms of meditation, but the one I mean entails focusing on the breath. Our minds wander, so in meditation, the objective is to focus on the breath. When you notice that your mind has wandered and you are no longer focusing on the breath, simply bring yourself back to focusing on the breath without judgment about your mind having wandered. The more you meditate, the more your meditating skills strengthen. This same technique can be used for developing mental skills.

This technique works for any mental skill, including patience. Patience is vital when learning new skills, because without patience, you'll want to have learned the skill immediately. Without patience, you'll give up after the first failure, or maybe after another—but give up you will.

Patience is the mixture of relaxation and faith. It's being relaxed during a situation when things are expected to happen immediately, with the full faith that everything will happen at the right time. You hear people say, "I just don't have the patience for this" or "You're testing my patience." First, if you want to learn a skill, positive self-talk is important. "I am learning how to improve my patience. This situation is an opportunity to learn patience." You develop patience, and all mental skills, through situations that require it.

Let's say you are at a restaurant and your food has taken a long time to arrive. You haven't eaten in hours, and the "hangry" in you is in full force, so you start to get flustered and think about taking it out on the server — who has no control over when your food is ready. When you notice your frustration, the same way you notice that your mind has wandered during meditation, remind yourself to relax and to think instead that the food is being prepared to perfection. In other words, bring yourself back to the breath without being flustered by judgment. This works for standing in lines, dealing with children, waiting for your significant other to propose, and any other situation in which you notice that you "want it now."

Every time you realize you are not being patient — or become aware of it — is a win. While learning new mental skills, every awareness is a win. It's like a set at the gym. Every time you catch yourself and change your thoughts, the stronger you become and the better you will be at that skill. So celebrate each win! Your brain will respond more when you get excited about each win, which leads to more wins. But it will also respond in the opposite direction if you beat yourself up. So try not to be judgmental toward yourself (also a skill), and celebrate the wins at garnering mental skills!

Patience is a vital skill to learn if we want to be able to learn other new skills. Without it, it's easy to give up on the things we want most. In fact, everything that's worth having is achieved through patience and effort. Whether it's a quality friendship, fulfillment, a long-term relationship, a career, success, or our ideal body, they all require patience and effort for them to mean anything. If they come overnight, what does that mean? Does that teach us anything? It's not the goal that matters, it's who we become in the process of achieving that goal that matters. The goal is just the reward for improving our life. Because if we don't change, we'll go right back to the bad habits that got us there in the first place. So the three skills we need to develop as a base foundation for our tool belt are cultivating beliefs, patience, and effort.

Effort comes from desire. We will not put any effort into anything unless we desire to do so, plain and simple. So in order to be able to put more effort into what we are trying to accomplish, we have to be able to link our actions with our desires. I have a desire and a passion to help others experience happiness and love in their lives, so I link that desire and passion into every action I take so I put more effort into it — even with the smallest of actions. Sometimes that means exercising and eating nutritiously so I have the energy to be able to do more. Other times it's putting myself in a better financial position so I have more money to help others in a more effective way. It's all about linking our desires with our efforts. This process of linking our desires with our actions is a mental skill. We have to become aware of our thinking during actions, and be able to link what we want most out of life with the actions we are taking.

We usually desire something for two reasons: to impress other people, or to have, do or be something that is true to who we are. The former is done out of fear of others' opinions, but the latter is done out of love for ourselves (and sometimes to share with others as well). Doing things out of fear leads to anger and hatred; doing things out of love leads to happiness and more love.

You may be in the job you have now because of society's standards or because that's what your parents wanted for you. Instead of following your heart, you decided to not let others down. But guess what that leads to? Anger towards your parents or others and hatred for your job, because doing things out of fear leads to anger and hatred. But if you follow your heart and go after the career you want for yourself, it will lead you to happiness and love for what you do. Your parents or others may be disappointed, but they will still love you. If they don't, then unfortunately they didn't love you in the first place, because love is not conditional. It would just mean they don't love themselves, because you cannot give what you do not have. Therefore, you cannot give love to others if you do not have love for yourself.

Most people who base their approval of you on what they want for your life actually do want you to succeed. The problem is that they are basing it on their own definitions of success and not yours. So you have to ask yourself, is your life worth living in fear, hatred and anger to please other people?

If the answer is no, find out what you want to do, and go after it! Learn the skills you need to learn to be the best you can be. Start with the three main skills: changing beliefs, effort and patience (check out the resource sections for developing these skills). Then figure out what skills you need to excel at the career you truly want. When you're choosing your career, don't worry about the money; think about what will make you happy. What job will allow you to express who you are?

You may temporarily have to be at a job you don't enjoy, but that pays the bills. Even then, don't lock yourself into making that your life plan simply because it will result in lots of money, because it's really not the money you're after. It's actually the financial freedom of not having to worry about money. The only way to have that freedom is to have faith in your ability to make money.

There are infinite ways to earn money. Your current job is just one of them. But if you work at a job that suppresses your individuality — who you are — you will hate it. We resent everything that doesn't allow us to be ourselves, including our jobs. The quickest way to find out if a job is going to suppress who you are is to look at a company's culture. Company culture is one of the most important aspects of a job that is right for you.

Almost every company, and big corporations in particular, understand the importance of company culture. What they don't understand is that the worst mistake they can make as a company is trying to force their employees to fit into their culture. Instead of hiring only people who fit their culture, they hire people who meet the job description and then force them into the company culture — usually with the fear of layoffs. Forcing people to be who they are not will always lead to resentment. Employees will resent their jobs and their employer. Resentment leads to low engagement, and low engagement leads to people not caring about their work at all. They'll do just enough to not get fired. So, please, don't become resentful; become happy. Pick a career and company that aligns with who you are.

When you look for a job, look at company culture. Ask about it during the interview. Also, if you can, talk to current employees about it, and try to meet your new boss beforehand. Make sure the culture and management style sounds like something that aligns with who you are. Otherwise, you'll be forced into their culture and you'll end up hating your job.

You will most likely spend eight hours at work and an hour to two hours commuting to and from it every day for five days out of the week, for nearly forty-five years. That's 105,000 hours of your life. Make sure you enjoy it! You shouldn't need a vacation from your life. Your life should be the vacation.

A lot of people want to be entrepreneurs because they tried working for someone else and hated it, or because being an independent entrepreneur looks "cool." Instead of looking for company culture that represents them, they try to start their own business. There's nothing wrong with that, but not everyone is meant to be a business owner.

After I quit my desk job, I came up with a social media app idea that would revolutionize the industry (or so I thought in my egotistical head). I wanted so badly to have the freedom of being my own boss. I was after the title of "Founder/CEO." I wanted to be in the craze of working in the startup industry. The app was called "Purpose," and it was basically an online support group for people with similar goals. Think Facebook groups, but with the added Tinder feature of matching people. For instance, let's say someone has the goal of beating a certain type of cancer, quitting cigarettes, losing weight or becoming sober. The app would match them with other people with the same goal and someone who had achieved that goal. It would also match parents of children with rare disabilities and the like so that they could support each other. This would allow a group of people to share their daily wins, struggles, and words of encouragement to help each other reach their goal.

I started learning the skills of a startup entrepreneur. I took coding classes. I took design classes. I watched startup classes. Eventually, after several months of wasted effort, I realized that I am not a social media entrepreneur. Yes, I wanted to help people with this app, but I was mainly after the fame, the money and the title. I found myself forcing it, which is usually an indication that what you are doing is not who you are. I decided that I was not a startup entrepreneur, and continued searching for my next passion, my next career move.

I do think it's a great app idea that could help a lot of people. If someone wants to take it, go for it. I'd be happy to give you more details. I did try messaging Mark Zuckerberg on Facebook to take the idea. So maybe instead of reading one of the gazillion messages he gets daily, he'll read my book and implement the feature into Facebook groups. This paragraph's for you, Zuck.

My point is that self-awareness is key. I should have given up on the app idea days into trying to learn skills that weren't meant for me to learn. Some skills take us longer to learn, while others can learn them very quickly. Just because we can learn any skill doesn't mean we should try and learn them all. It just means we get to pick and choose any skill that allows us to excel at being who we are.

If you learn the skills that will allow you to excel at your job, or the new job you want, then the money will come easily — especially when you also learn money skills. When you learn money skills, you'll become able to learn the skill of investing. And I recommend your investments also represent who you are.

If you believe that social media is destroying the world, but have stocks in Facebook, Twitter, Snapchat and the like, that tells me you care more about money than you do your own beliefs. Investments are more rewarding when they are aligned with your beliefs and with who you are, because you are rooting for their purpose and not just the money it makes you.

If you don't know what skills to learn, there is a resource in the back of this book that lists recommended skills. Look them over and see which skills you can work on. The more skills you develop, the more money you'll earn. Buffet was right: the more you learn the more you earn. The more you earn, the more freedom you'll have to express who you are — in every area of your life.

Although there are many skills that will help you on your journey through life, there is usually a skill or a skill set that you are naturally good at, perhaps without even knowing it. In other words, there are skills that you are a *genius* at.

CHAPTER NINE

Find Your Genius

"Everyone is a genius. But if you judge a fish by its ability to climb a tree, it will live its whole life believing that it is stupid."

– Albert Einstein, Genius

This has to be one of my favorite quotes of all time. Have you grasped its *significance*? When most people see quotes like this, they hear the words but miss the wisdom. If you don't see the importance of this quote, let me help to explain it.

THE GENIUS OF ALL GENIUSES SAID THAT EVERYONE IS A GENIUS. THAT INCLUDES YOU.

A man whose name is synonymous with genius thinks that you are a genius. What about you? Do you think you're a genius?

If your first thought is "No," it is because of the quotation's second sentence. Every single person on this beautiful planet is unique.

Just like every animal species is unique, so is each individual human. So maybe you can be likened to a fish. Maybe your genius lies in swimming, not climbing a tree.

Our education system today tells us we are "smart" if we get high grades. Mainly when we are children, society tells us that in order to be successful, we must do well in school. The higher the grade, the greater the likelihood of success. In other words, they judge our genius on our ability to climb trees. Not everyone is good at math. Not everyone is a fanatic about language arts. A person who is not good at math could be a genius at dancing on Broadway. A person who is not passionate about language arts could be a genius at building things and working with their hands.

The sad part is that most people never find their genius. They have submitted to the false premise that genius lies exclusively in subjects our education system teaches. So instead of relentlessly persisting to find their genius, they settle for what they think they can do. They settle for mediocre. Or, worse, they settle for what society wants them to do. Society says, "Be an engineer, doctor or lawyer, because that's where the real money is." But where is the happiness? It's within your genius. If you hate what you do for income, it's an indication that you are not using your natural gifts, your very own genius.

We are all geniuses at something. Whether that's math and science, diagnosing patients, baking, networking, singing to the crowds, or anything else, we are all geniuses at something. But our genius doesn't lie only in the skills we are good at; our genius lies in our creativity with the skills we are good at.

We are all creative beings. Creativity is a skill. The more you use your creativity, the better you get at it. But if you have the belief that you aren't creative, do you think you'll ever exercise your creativity? Of course not! You won't even know it's there. Creativity isn't only in art forms; it lies in every skill there is.

Creativity means the use of imagination to create new or original ideas. You can be creative in your kindness to others. You can be creative in your ability to exercise patience. You can be creative in anything you do, be it marketing, throwing a baseball, cooking or even mathematics.

Creativity is one of the very few skills that make us all human. When we submit to the false premise that we aren't creative, it kills a little sense of who we are. Our genius is one of the reasons we are here in the first place. It's how we have the ability to change the world—big or small. Movie stars' genius lies in acting. Pop stars' genius lies in singing and entertaining. They have this gift, which they probably have worked extremely hard to master, to help bring entertainment to the world. Storytelling and music are how people can connect with each other, which is why it creates celebrities.

Celebrities can use their genius to put themselves into the spotlight. Then they can either hide behind the mask of the way society wants them to behave, or they can be themselves and focus on the positive change they wish to create in the world. In a world in which everyone is criticized for things they do or don't do, most celebrities feel trapped in a box, one that determines how they have to behave in order to get fans. Any public criticism could cost them their fame, reputation or fortune, so instead, they pretend to be who they are not. You can see this in celebrity overdoses. These celebrities feel that the only way out of the box is to leave the body. But this is only because they forgot why their genius was given to them in the first place. It's not to show people how to live in a box, but to show people how they can soar and how to use their creative genius to make an impact on the world.

When you use your genius to be yourself, to help other people along the way, the result is positive change within the world. No matter how big or small, positive change is positive change, and everyone born wants to feel like they have left this place better than when they found it. And that all starts with finding your genius.

A good way to look for your genius is by asking yourself, "What skills/subjects do I love to learn or learn about?" Maybe you are obsessed with flowers. Your genius may lie in how to grow flowers creatively. Do you love sports? What is it about sports that you love? Is it the statistics? Maybe your genius lies in providing the world with different types of statistics. The examples are endless, but only you know in your heart what you love to learn about. It doesn't matter how silly or odd it may sound to other people. All that matters is if *you* are the one who loves to learn about it.

Sometimes that might mean getting outside your comfort zone to try new things. Maybe it's getting outside your comfort zone to re-try the things you failed at before. Maybe you lied to yourself that you just weren't good at it because failing was uncomfortable. Your comfort zone is a tight, safe bubble that prevents you from trying new things and makes you think failing means failure. If you don't try new things or give up after failure, how can you ever find your genius? You can't.

What if Lebron James never picked up a basketball or gave up after failing at one practice? Or what if he *only* played basketball instead of using his natural genius to speak out to create positive change in the world (which includes a free public school that guarantees college tuition upon graduation)? Or, worse, what if Steve Jobs never picked up a computer? If Jobs had conformed to society's expectations, he would have finished school at Stanford instead. With a college degree, would he still have taken the risks to help create Apple, which brought technology to the world? Or, would he play it safe and get a corporate job like the rest of his classmates? Or even more frightening, what if Martin Luther King, Jr., never picked up a microphone? Where would our society be if MLK, Jr. decided to do what others told him to do instead of leading the civil rights movement — a movement that is still trying to unify a nation to this day?

The people who have gone on to change the world are people who have decided to ignore society's expectations of conformity. If you do not want to change the world, then change your world, because positively changing your world *is* changing the world. To do that, you must be able to break through your comfort zone, which means you have to develop the skill of courage.

"The opposite of courage in
today's society is not cowardice; it is conformity."

– Rollo May, Psychologist

CHAPTER TEN

The Mask of Comfort

"Life begins at the end of your comfort zone."

– Neale Donald Walsch, *NY Times* **Best-Selling Author**

Our lives are a direct reflection of the choices we have made. Some people think that the future is pre-determined, that no matter what we do, the same circumstances will arise. If the future is pre-determined, then why are we here? Why go through all of this if the outcome is fixed? And why do we have free will? If the future is pre-determined, then we wouldn't have free will at all. All of our choices would be set for us.

The only way your future is pre-determined is if you keep making the same choices. You know what your life will be like if you keep making those same choices; you're already living it. Choices can be the people we hang out with, our career, our internal dialogue, our appearance, the skills we learn and the exercises we do or do not do. The list of choices is endless. Most of us keep making the same choices, which is why our lives stay the same. Usually we make the choice of mental comfort — where we feel certain of our actions' outcomes and in control of our lives. We choose what is comfortable instead of what might be uncertain.

There is a huge difference between being happy and being comfortable. Comfort is one of the hideous masks we wear, but instead of showing it to the world, we wear it in front of the mirror. Comfort is actually fear, disguised as an excuse not to *do*. The "do" I'm talking about is that little nudge within you that tells you to do something you haven't done before. It's your true self trying to express a bigger and better version of *you*. But instead of listening to that little nudge, comfort-oriented thinking usually takes over. "You might get hurt. What if you get rejected? You'll fail anyway. What will other people think of you? You know what happens if you don't do it. It can't get worse than it is now if you don't go through with it."

The actual thoughts are probably different, but the line of thinking is the same. If you don't listen to that inner nudge, you know where your life will be. You're already experiencing it. This line of thinking that claims there is certainty staying where you're at is fear, disguised as comfort.

The problem is that without making a change, your life will be the same! You can't improve your life if you remain the same. Whatever that little nudge within is telling you to do—sure, you may fail; you may get rejected; it may not go as planned—but maybe that's the point! Maybe your true self wants you to learn how to deal with failure, rejection, and uncertainty. Even if what you "do" doesn't go the way you want it to, your life will improve. Why? Because you will have learned a lesson from it. You will have learned how to deal with other challenges you may face on the road ahead, which is the best kind of improvement there is.

When I started out on my "Lone Wolf" journey, it was extremely uncomfortable. I had never been alone in my entire life. I grew up in a very close family in which we were always around each other. After I graduated from high school and went to college, I always had roommates. After college, I lived with my former fiancée. Eventually, like a lot of people who end up in long-term relationships, I became comfortable. I started to gain weight, never met new people out of fear of rejection, and did nothing but go to work or stay in the comfort of my own home. I never wanted to do anything else. The mask of comfort was glued to my face.

When my former fiancée finally moved out, I was all alone. I had two choices: sulk in loneliness or get out of my comfort zone and meet new people. At first, I chose to sulk. I used to swipe on Tinder, Bumble, E-harmony, Match and every other online dating site you can think of. Instead of going out and facing the possibility of rejection, I spent hundreds of dollars on "boosts" and premium accounts to have a better shot at meeting someone online. This was when I was still overweight, so I had no confidence either.

Then one day, while I was walking my dog, that little nudge hit me. I was trying to think of ways to improve my life and how to get out of this state of loneliness and borderline depression. Suddenly, a random thought popped into my head: "Send a message to some of my fraternity brothers, forgiving them for abandoning me and rejecting me from entering the frat house." Comfort mode immediately kicked in. "What? That's ridiculous. It's been almost six years. Who still cares? I don't even care that much. They're just going to think I'm weak if they know it even mattered to me. This is silly and it makes no sense. How will this improve my life and get me to the next stage? Nope, I'm not doing it." The excuses fear drew out went on and on.

Usually, when we decide we aren't going to do the "do," we start to feel relaxed. Then we stop thinking about it, especially if it's something that could only have been done in that moment. But this was different; it was something I had the opportunity to do anytime. And the nudge wouldn't go away; it was almost as strong as the glue of my mask. Eventually, I thought, "Why do I care what they think? I will never see them again." So I wrote three messages to my old fraternity brothers. Two of the messages flat-out said, "I forgive you for always kicking me out of the house." The other thanked that person for teaching me some valuable lessons I had taken for granted when he first taught me.

The sky didn't fall. My life didn't go backwards. In fact, it was the catalyst that caused me to write this book. It made me realize that other people's opinions don't matter at all; that the fear was only in my head. I started to listen to the nudge, over and over again. I eventually started going out to bars by myself, something I wouldn't do before because I didn't want to look like a loner.

One night I was feeling lonely, and I started to message all of my old high school and college buddies. It was uncomfortable because I hadn't talked to any of them in over five years, and the possibility of rejection was high. Most of them didn't respond. Some of them did, but the conversations didn't go anywhere — except with one friend.

He invited me to a bar where he knew someone who was playing in a live band. I went, and met a bunch of his old friends from high school whom he had invited there as well. One of them was this beautiful girl whom I hadn't met before. We talked for maybe five minutes that night. The next morning the nudge hit me again: "Add her on Facebook and ask her out on a date." So I did, even though I could have easily been rejected. To my delight, she said yes. We set a date for two weeks later based on our schedules. In those two weeks, I started to become very depressed. I was sleeping and lying in bed for over sixteen hours a day. I felt as if I had no purpose, no direction, and had no idea what to do next. As the date slowly approached, I decided not to text her and let our date fall apart. After the date had passed, the depression hit a very scary all-time low.

I wasn't sure what was going to happen next, so I decided to meditate to calm my mind. After I meditated, the nudge had hit me again. "Write her a poem apologizing and asking her back out on a date." I wrestled with it, but I would have done anything to get myself out of what I was experiencing. So I wrote the poem and sent it to her. She thought it was cute and agreed to set a new date.

Listening to that nudge was exactly what I had needed to lift my spirits. It sparked a new energy in me that allowed me to change directions, which made me feel confident and alive to continue to keep listening to it.

We went on the date, and I thought we had a great time, so I asked her out again on another date. This time, I was rejected. She told me she thought I was cool, but that it would be best if we just spent time in groups.

It stung, but at least she was honest and didn't drag it out. A couple days later, I saw on Facebook that she needed players for her kickball team. The nudge hit me again. "Ask her if I could play on her kickball team." The excuses of fear poured in. "Kickball? I played that in elementary school. That's silly. Plus, she just rejected me! It'll be so awkward! I thought I was never going to see her again!" At this point, I knew what was going on. I had felt so alive from getting out of my comfort zone before, there was no way I was going to let fear get in my way. So I asked her, and I played on her kickball team. Six months later, we started dating. It has since ended, but she taught me so much about myself that it was worth every second of the relationship.

As the year continued, I started listening to the nudge over and over again. Since I decided to lean in to my true self, I went from complete loneliness and isolation to now having friends from all over the world. I went from having doubts and worries to now having the confidence to do anything I set my mind to. But most importantly, I went from being depressed and insecure to now fully in love with myself — and experiencing the habitual happiness that comes with it.

This all started with three silly messages to people whose opinions I was afraid of. If I hadn't sent those messages, I wouldn't have experienced the excitement of breaking out of my comfort zone. I wouldn't have met an amazing woman who taught me so much about myself. I wouldn't have gone to that bar by myself that night and had the epiphany about the cycle of approval. And you wouldn't be reading this book as you are right now. I could have *chose* differently, and I'm so grateful I didn't.

My life has improved in ways that used to seem inconceivable — all because I trusted that little nudge from within. I decided to lean in to my true self, which was there all along, waiting for me outside my comfort zone.

They say life begins at the end of your comfort zone. But is it really *life* that begins, or is it the *purpose of your life* that begins at the end of your comfort zone? People talk about purpose a lot. They want to feel that their lives have meaning, a purpose. The truth is, you do have a purpose—we all do, and it's waiting for you at the end of your comfort zone. Your purpose isn't handed to you; you're led to it. It's that little nudge from within that says, "Do." The "do" may seem so small and ridiculous that it is not even worth getting uncomfortable for. But how can you do something uncomfortable that you consider to be big if you can't do something that is small? Getting uncomfortable and being courageous is a skill—a skill, like a muscle, that gets stronger the more you exercise it.

Being courageous by getting outside of your comfort zone will always lead you to your purpose. Sometimes your purpose isn't what you do; it's what you learn from what you do, no matter what age you are. Your purpose isn't a single event. No matter how young or old you think you are, your purpose is an evolving process that inspires you to do more: to love more, help more, have more and, ultimately, be more.

It is human nature to want more. People sometimes tell us to be satisfied with what we have and who we are, but being satisfied goes against every fiber of our being, and the result is a mask of comfort. We should always be happy and grateful for what we have and who we are—but never satisfied. There's always room for improvement in every aspect of our lives. This doesn't mean we have to be a perfectionist, but it does mean that we should never be satisfied. Satisfaction leads to mediocrity. Doing the do leads to purpose.

The only way to be more, to continually fulfill our purpose, is to expand our comfort zones. Take a look below:

The ring is your comfort zone, or the habitual choices that you are used to making. The dot is the "do," or the nudge from within

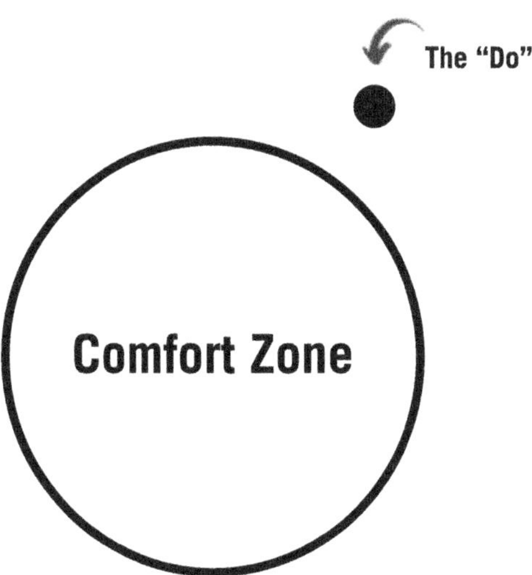

that wants you to break free from your habitual choices. When you get the nudge to "do," you'll probably hit a wall of fear and excuses disguised as comfort. Do it anyway. Courage isn't the absence of fear, but doing the "do" in the face of fear. When you do the do, your comfort zone will start to expand, and you'll be comfortable doing more things. See below:

When you feel the fear and proceed anyway, your comfort zone expands to the spot of the "do." It may take several times for your

comfort zone to expand in a lasting way, but each time it will get easier. The beautiful thing about expanding your comfort zone is that you're now able to do more things.

Let's say the nudge tells you to join a public speaking class, something you're terrified of doing. You do it anyway, and you start to give speeches. It may take several speeches to become comfortable, but eventually your comfort zone expands.

When you expand your comfort zone in this way, you may now not only be comfortable giving speeches, but you will also feel comfortable getting up in front of a crowd. Maybe you're actually a singer, musician or entertainer who hasn't quite found your genius yet. If you are, you become comfortable getting in front of a crowd because of having followed your nudge from within, doing the do, and expanding your comfort zone. The nudge may then lead you to taking singing lessons, guitar lessons or acting classes. As you continually follow the nudge, your comfort zone expands, and your purpose continually unfolds.

What is the nudge? Well, what the nudge is not is peer pressure. People sometimes want you to do something you know you shouldn't. The nudge in that case will tell you *not* to do what the outside world is telling you to do. The nudge, which always wants you to expand the quality of your life, always comes from within. This could mean the outside world is encouraging you to do something, and the nudge tells you to follow through. It's all about listening to what is inside of you—what you are feeling about the situation.

The nudge is your intuition. It's what people mean when they say, "Follow your heart" or "Listen to your gut." It has been said that prayer is us talking to God, and our intuition is God talking to us. Logic and reasoning can only get us so far, because they are based on our knowledge alone, which is limited to our own experiences. When compared to how many possible experiences there are, that isn't a whole lot.

Our intuition is a part of what connects us all. It's one of the many links between us that knows the path to take, the path that aligns us with our purpose. We may not always know the results that will come from acting on our intuitions, which is why it can be scary, but intuition always leads us to bigger and better things. Acting on my intuition started with sending three simple messages, which was a very scary thing for me to do at the time. Now it's expanded my life's purpose to something greater than myself.

The root of the word courage is "cor"—which is the Latin word for heart. Courage is listening to your heart, despite all the fears and excuses that come from your head. Someone once said that courage comes from confidence. You have to have confidence in yourself in order to be habitually courageous—otherwise your lack of faith in yourself will outweigh your desires. Unfortunately, confidence also comes from courage. You have to be able to do something courageous in order to have the confidence that you *can* do it. They are intertwined.

So you will have to make a decision. You can either wait until you have the confidence to act (which may never happen), or you can choose to act just that one time. Make a decision that you will feel the fear and do it anyway. Listen to your nudge just that first time, do the do, and then start to gain confidence. When you keep acting by doing the do, you will begin to gain more and more confidence to tackle your fears. Instead of living a life out of fear of other people's opinions, which are created in your head, you will live a life that matches no other. You will live a life that is destined for only you.

Like everything else in life, breaking through your comfort zone and acting on your intuition is a skill. It takes patience and effort, and the more you do it, the better you'll get at it. You can live your whole life in fear, disguised as comfort, and come to the end of your life with the regrets of "what if"; or, you can just do the do, getting to the end of your life with the fulfillment of purpose.

I choose purpose. I choose the do.

CHAPTER ELEVEN

Your Most Surprising Teacher

"Ego can be the great success inhibitor.
It can kill opportunities and it can kill success."

– Dwayne "The Rock" Johnson, Actor

Dwayne is completely right, but only if we decide to *act* from our ego. But our ego doesn't have to be a success inhibitor; in fact, our ego can be one of our greatest teachers. We can make decisions based on ego, or we can learn from our ego.

Ego, as I describe it in this chapter, is another word for insecurity. An insecurity is an area of our life that we feel unloved, uncertain, or inadequate. The reason we have insecurities is because other people have made us feel unloved in those areas of our lives. We then become afraid that other people will use those insecurities against us, and we'll be left to feel unloved when they do. Most people do not want to admit that they have insecurities, or that they have an ego — meaning they have an insecurity about having insecurities. And you can't blame them. In a world where everyone is trying to be better than everyone else, it can be very difficult to admit that you have insecurities. That's because insecurities are seen as weaknesses. But the truth is, we all have them, and when we don't admit that we have them, we don't even realize they're there.

Is there anything that happens within your relationships — family, friends, or lover(s)—that consistently upsets you? If so, I invite you to see if there is an insecurity hiding within. It's not the weakness we know about that causes us to fail. It's the weakness we don't know about that will lead to our ultimate downfall.

Insecurities can come from anywhere — all of them lies we've bought into. Maybe our parents made us feel as though we weren't good enough. Maybe society made us feel as if we weren't attractive enough. Maybe our friends made us feel as if we weren't smart enough. Whatever the case may be, the first step to healing insecurities is to admit that we have them. Otherwise, we'll always act differently because of them, which will become our success inhibitor.

Success born out of ego is always impossible because it will never heal our insecurities. It will only bury them deeper. The ego always wants more. Our true self does too, but there is a major difference between the two.

Your true self wants more for yourself. Your true self wants more titles specifically so you can build a bigger following and make a bigger impact on the world. Your true self wants more money so you can enjoy financial freedom and help others along the way. Your true self wants more adventure to feel alive and to create the feeling of excitement. Your true self wants more so you can be more.

The ego is the complete and total opposite. The ego wants more titles to seem more important than other people. The ego wants more money to seem better and more successful than others. The ego wants more adventure to post on social media. The ego wants more of things to hide our insecurities, but hiding never heals anything. The motive behind every desire comes either from ego or from a place of true self. The motive behind our every desire comes either from an insecurity or from a place of love.

The ego wants people to like you. Your true self already loves you. The ego has expectations of what other people should do. Your true self has expectations of what *you* should do.

When we expect things from others, it can lead to disappointment if they don't behave how we expected them to. Habitual disappointment leads to resentment. When we expect things from ourselves, and we follow through, it leads to accomplishments. It leads to achievements. Not in the sense of, "Look at what I've done," but for the feeling of fulfillment and purpose that comes from becoming more than we once were.

Someone once said that the ego stands for "Edge God Out." But if that's the case, then the ego should really be called EPO — "Edge People Out." The main reason why making decisions from the ego is a success inhibitor is that our ego drives the people we love out of our life, usually because we misinterpret what the people in our lives say or do. We only see their actions through our Reticular Activating System, which filters our experience by what we believe. If we have insecurities (which we all do), we sometimes view other people's actions through some of those misconceived beliefs we have about ourselves. Most of the time, people don't do or say things with the intent that we think they do, and when we act from that misinterpretation, we can end up driving them out.

The ego even drives the people we don't know yet, who could become our great friends, out of our lives. When we do things just to get ahead of others, people sense our arrogance, and people don't want to feel like we are better than they are. We are all created equal. Just because some people don't act like it doesn't make it untrue.

The biggest indication of ego in action is anger towards others. Don't confuse anger with frustration. Frustration comes from forcing things that are not meant to be. Frustration is an indication that you are on the wrong path and it would be a good time to pivot. Anger towards others comes from an insecurity being exposed. It is in times of anger that your biggest opportunity for growth emerges.

When I was designing the cover of this book, one of my good friends showed it to one of her friends for feedback. Her friend said, "He shouldn't have his face on the cover. People are going to say, 'What does this young-looking white kid know about being yourself?' And then they will not buy the book."

I was livid. But thankfully, I understood that this was meant to be constructive criticism and that I was only angry because it was a huge slap to my ego. So I was honest with myself — that there was a reason for my getting angry. I was being shown an opportunity to grow and to heal a major insecurity I thought I might have had. I vented my anger to my friend because it's important to feel through your emotions, not suppress them. But I did it by first acknowledging in a calm tone that I understood that this had been a slap to my ego, that I understood that my anger came from an insecurity of my own, and not from what her friend had actually said. This allowed her to not get defensive and to understand that this was something I was working through.

After the anger had subsided, I started to ponder why I was so upset. And then it hit me. The major insecurity I had was that people wouldn't believe in me because I used to believe that my parents didn't believe in me. The truth is that my parents do believe in me. I just take their constructive criticism and advice the wrong way because they are my parents and it's hard to take criticism from people you love. But in the end, it doesn't matter if anyone believes in me; all that matters is that I believe in myself. As I realized that, I was able to shift my thinking from that of needing the approval of others to needing the approval of the only person who matters, which is me. I decided to keep my face on the cover because it represents me being myself. And, after all, that's what this book is all about.

Through my ego, I was able turn an insecurity into a strength. I could have missed the opportunity for growth. I could have taken my anger out on my friend and her friend. I could have ended up hating her friend when she was only trying to help me. I could have changed the cover design because of someone else's opinion. But, worst of all, I could have edged my friend out.

It may not happen the first time, but every decision we make out of ego further drives a wedge between the people we care about and ourselves. After too many of those times, the space becomes too big, and we can lose those people forever.

Another way to discover where an insecurity lies is to ask yourself, what area of your life do you feel the need for the most security? The areas in life that we need the most security on the outside are usually the areas in life that we are the most insecure on the inside.

If we feel the need for financial security, then we are most likely insecure about finances. That can show up as being extremely frugal, people hoarding money, or clinging to a job they hate. If we feel the need for fame, titles, or to feel important, we are most likely insecure about our self-worth. That can show up in our determination to work long hours to get promoted, in our decisions to keep getting degrees that we don't need, or even just needing others to validate our self-worth. If we feel the need for romantic security, we may be insecure about our ability to be loved by others. That can show up as being needy, wanting more attention, or being jealous when our significant other is talking to someone of the same sex as us.

All insecurities come from other people — the environments we were raised in, the people we hung around, or what we were bullied for in school or even in our later years. If we were raised with frugal parents or in a poor family, then we are most likely to be insecure about finances because our parents probably were too. If we consistently felt like we were never good enough for our parents, society, etc., it's probably because our parents or the people we hung around didn't feel as if they were good enough either. The reasons for insecurities and examples are endless, but they are always on us to heal them. As Will Smith once said, just because something is someone else's fault doesn't mean that it isn't our responsibility to fix it. Insecurities are merely a cycle of people projecting them onto other people, and it is up to us to break that cycle.

Is it possible for us to give what we do not have? Of course the answer is no, so why do we think we can give love to others if we do not have love for ourselves? Why do we expect other people to give us love if they do not have love for themselves? We all have different areas in life where we love ourselves, and others where we do not. If we cannot give what we do not have, then other people cannot give us love in an area of life in which they do not have love for themselves. If all they have are insecurities in those areas, then that is all they can give us.

Insecurities usually show up in our determination to be considered successful in some area of life — especially if it's just one area. But the word successful has a "ful" at the end of it — meaning true success comes from being *full* of success in all areas of our lives. Hidden insecurities that show up as a determination to succeed doesn't apply to our passion or to what we love doing; it applies to the areas in life in which we want others to think something about us, and only ourselves know the difference.

As I mentioned in a previous chapter, I had a tough time being confident around girls when I was in high school. That changed when I lost weight and gained confidence. I was now able to be confident around women, but because I never truly healed the insecurity, I was still very insecure about dating women — meaning I felt the need for romantic security.

In a previous relationship, that insecurity came out. I felt the need to spend more and more time with her, which only drove her further away. I tried putting 100% of my effort into the relationship, and ignored most of the other areas of my life.

Eventually, I edged her out, and because I was able to realize and *acknowledge* that, I have been able to heal an insecurity that will help me in the future — with romantic relationships and with all other areas of my life. I can now give more attention to the balance of life instead of trying to force feeling that sense of love from my romantic partner.

It's not easy to acknowledge our insecurities, and it may take some time to heal them, and that's okay. Just know that every time you realize and acknowledge you have an insecurity that needs to be healed, you're already on your way. Find the root cause of the insecurity. Who or what made you believe this about yourself? Then use the principles from the mirror of love to turn your insecurities into love, and learn to love yourself wholeheartedly. If the root of an insecurity is an experience of trauma from your past, then I would recommend seeking a professional to help in your healing.

When you are able to heal your insecurities and develop a strong, foundational love and confidence for yourself, people's comments will cease to irritate you, and your ego will quickly dissolve. Then you can start to achieve true balance in your life. Balance is the key to a fulfilling life, but our insecurities prevent us from achieving that balance. Instead, we focus on trying to fill the void of feeling unloved.

An insecurity may not seem like an area that is "unloved"

when it is getting exposed, especially for men. That's probably because some people, mostly men, equate love with respect — or what they consider to be approval. When they feel that sense of disrespect or rejection from the people they love (or even a stranger), their anger can come out in full force. And then their actions can lead to edging the people they care about out. But there is only one person in the entire universe whose respect you truly need, and that is your own.

This sense of demanding respect from others can lead to one of the deadliest diseases that has ever existed, and that disease is called stubbornness. Being stubborn is the result of when people demand respect in the form of always being considered right. In reality, it's not that they have to be right — they just fear being considered wrong.

Stubbornness is a disease that can kill our relationships, our finances, and our chances to grow and love ourselves — all three areas in which we can exercise our habitual happiness. We can be stubborn with holding grudges, always bringing them up or never fully forgiving other people — which edges those people out and creates a feeling of hatred instead of love. We can be stubborn with our finances, pricing our products or services too high because of what we believe we should get for it and not based on what the market is willing to pay — which edges money right out of our lives. And we can be stubborn with our beliefs, demanding that all of our beliefs are true without ever considering the alternative—edging out the new ideas that could positively change our lives forever. The examples of stubbornness in each of these three areas are endless, but the results are always the same: edging out the happiness we so rightfully deserve.

When people say, "You can't fix stupid," what they are really saying is, "You can't fix stubborn." No one is inherently stupid, unless they are choosing to be through their stubbornness. Stubbornness is born out of ego — out of insecurity. When you have nothing but total, true love for yourself, you don't need to always be right. You understand that we are all here to grow, learn, and improve, and that it is completely okay to be wrong. Our self-esteem doesn't come from always being right or tearing others down to feel right. Our self-worth and self-esteem comes from building ourselves up, and the only way to do that is to learn as much as we possibly can — especially how to love ourselves.

There is a difference between being strong-willed and being stubborn. Being stubborn is a fear of being wrong. Being strong-willed is saying, "My core values are important to me, and no one can force me to act without them." Being strong-willed is about staying true to who you are, and not allowing anyone to change you unless it aligns with more of who you are. When you are being strong-willed, you don't need to seem right to other people — you only care about being right to yourself. Our intentions always matter. They either come from our true self, or from that of the ego.

The ego isn't who we are. It's the result of our insecurities, which are just misguided beliefs about ourselves that other people had us believe. Our true selves love everything about us, so when our beliefs about who we are and what we are capable of align with our true selves, there is nothing to be insecure about. Understood in this way, the ego becomes a teacher that leads us to our true self — but only if we decide to shift our thinking about our insecurities.

Improving our lives is never-ending. We can always have, do and be more as long as we do it from a place that represents our true selves and not our egos. However, the only way to come from a place that represents our true selves is to practice the skill of authenticity.

CHAPTER TWELVE

The Skill of Authenticity

"Honesty is the best policy."

- Benjamin Franklin,
Founding Father of The United States of America

Honesty is a skill. It's really the only skill you need to be authentically you. I'm not talking about haphazard honesty, where you get to pick and choose the situations in which you are honest. I'm talking about complete and total honesty *all* the time.

Ugly masks come from lying — lying to others, but mainly lying to ourselves, especially in front of others. It's easy to lie. It's easy to lie to avoid uncomfortable situations or to save someone from getting their feelings hurt. It's easy to lie and tell ourselves, "I'm doing this for me," when really, we're probably doing it for our mother or our friends or anyone other than ourselves.

Living a life for others is not being honest. It's lying to everyone around us, saying, "This is who I am" when in reality it's, "This is who I'm pretending to be." A lot of people think that doing things for themselves is selfish, but there's a huge difference between living a life for others and living a life to *serve* others. We're sometimes raised to always "do things for others," and feel that doing anything else is considered selfish. But that's completely untrue. Being selfish is asking, "What's in it for me?" Being selfless is asking, "How may I serve?"

The honest answer to the latter question may be to say, "No, I will not do that for you. I have to focus on myself right now, so that I can get better, in order to serve more people." You can't serve anyone if you are living a life for others. Living a life for others keeps you small. Living a life for yourself, so that you may serve more people, makes you soar.

The only way to keep soaring is to adopt the skill of complete and total honesty in everything you do. We all lie at some point in our lives. A fake laugh is a lie—a small lie, but a lie nonetheless. It's saying, "I know you're trying to be funny. You're not funny, but I don't want you to feel bad about not being funny, so here's a fake laugh. Haha!" This gives people the false impression that what they said was funny. Instead of saying, "That just wasn't that funny, but good try though!" they now believe what they said was funny, and are more inclined to say it again. So, instead of helping that person not look like a fool again, we made the situation comfortable. It's a silly example, but it applies to almost every lie we tell in uncomfortable situations.

It's almost as if lying becomes an automatic response. I do it without thinking too sometimes. The skill of honesty is not just about never lying; it's about correcting your lie when it happens. It's being aware that you lied, admitting you lied and correcting yourself with the truth.

It can be extremely uncomfortable to admit you lied to someone. Lying is heavily frowned upon, as it should be. In fact, in today's culture of, "If you make one mistake, your whole life should be ruined," lying even once can mark you as a dishonest person. So to admit you lied takes a lot of courage.

Sometimes we lie to strangers to impress them, or we exaggerate the truth. We lie to friends so that they won't feel bad. We lie to acquaintances to avoid the awkwardness of turning down invitations. We lie to ourselves when we say that we are people-pleasers, when really we are just afraid of losing the approval of others and the fake feeling of love that comes with it.

But the only way to be authentically you is to always tell the truth, especially when you have just lied. If you don't correct the lie, there's a piece of a mask that stays with you — a piece that may seem comforting, but is actually saying, "I'm afraid of the uncomfortable."

Lying keeps you in a place you are not meant to be, spending time with people who are not right for you and doing things you were not meant to do. If you believe that we all have a purpose, do you really think you're on the path of purpose by lying? Lying is the one thing that will always steer you onto the wrong path.

When the Vegas trip happened and I didn't marry the woman I had planned to, I knew the relationship wasn't meant to be. In fact, I probably knew deep within before that that it wasn't meant to be. I just lied to myself because I loved her, I didn't want to hurt her, and I was scared of what life would be like without her. When I realized I was lying to myself, I then chose to lie to her instead. I stayed for almost a year more because I still loved her, but I felt obligated to stay. I felt obligated because she had always been there for me, no matter what, in every dark moment of my life. I truly loved her, and I still love her to this day—purely as a friend, but love her nonetheless. I couldn't face the discomfort of ending our relationship, so instead of telling the truth, I cowered in the lie.

The reason the relationship never would have worked had nothing to do with her. It was because I got comfortable with her—so comfortable that I was never really forced out of my comfort zone. Lying then became comfortable. This delayed my "Lone Wolf" journey of inner growth, and it delayed my purpose. The only way we can discover our purpose is to get out of our comfort zone and quit lying to people, including ourselves.

What is it that you are lying about? Is it your self-image? Your relationships? Your job? Doing things for other people's approval is lying to the outside world, pretending that we are someone we're not. Doing things strictly for others is lying to ourselves, thinking that other people's happiness is more important than our own. Spending time with people we don't like is lying to them, pretending that we actually enjoy their company. Spending time with people we don't like is lying to ourselves, trying to convince ourselves that their approval is more important than being on the path we were meant to be on. Working at a job we hate just for the money is lying to our employer that we want to be there. Working at a job we hate for the money is lying to ourselves that making money is more important than our happiness.

The truth is that our happiness is all that matters, because we can't control the happiness of others. The truth is that our happiness is more important than lots of money, because all of that money isn't worth having if we aren't happy. The truth is that being on the path we were meant to be on is more important than other people's approval. Our path lies in our ability to help serve others, not to be someone we aren't in the interests of others.

The skill of honesty is one of the most important skills we can build to live a life of authenticity and habitual happiness. It may not always take us on the most comfortable path, but it will always lead us down the right path. And it all starts with correcting our lies when we tell them. Even small lies should be corrected, because they get us into a bad habit. Lying about small things only makes it easier to lie about the big things.

Happiness comes from the feeling of loving yourself, and that means you have to be yourself. Being yourself is only possible with complete and total honesty. There are so many forms of lying that we can fall victim to. We sometimes lie about our emotions, our excuses, and in our communications with others.

Suppressing our emotions is actually lying to ourselves. It's us saying, "It is uncomfortable to feel this way. I don't want to feel this way. I'm going to force feeling another way by distracting myself." When we suppress these emotions, they don't go away. They build up until we can't suppress them any longer.

On one of my birthdays during college, my mother gave me one hundred dollars all in twenty-dollar bills. I was having lunch with a bunch of my family members, when I noticed a twenty-dollar bill was missing. I asked my mom how much she had given me, and she said one hundred dollars. She then gave me another twenty because we thought she had given me eighty by mistake. When one of the younger members of the family and I were alone together, that person admitted they had taken a twenty, knowing my mother would replace it. I would get the full one hundred dollars, and they would get twenty dollars.

I scolded them. I told them how wrong it is to steal, and that our family doesn't do things like that. That our integrity was everything. They were very young, mid-teens perhaps, and this was just a lesson they had to learn. But instead of feeling my way through the anger, understanding that it was a lesson for them and also forgiving them, I bottled up the emotion. From that point on, every time I saw that person, I reminded myself that they had stolen from me. I kept the anger bottled up and did not say anything about it.

One day, almost a year later, we all went to the house of a family friend for a pool party. I got completely drunk, and that family member was there—seeming much older now, driving a car. I had still kept the bottled-up anger in me. When I got drunk, my inhibitions dropped, and I let loose on that family member. I went completely ballistic and embarrassed myself and the other person in front of a group of people. I had lied to myself about my emotions by not feeling through them, and the result was an incident that scarred both of us. After that, I dealt with my emotions while sober, and decided to let it go and to forgive that person. We are now at a place where we have forgiven each other for what we both did, and we are both now very good friends.

When we suppress our emotions, it doesn't just affect us; it also affects the people around us. It's like holding onto a hand grenade with no timer: the longer we hold it, the more of a blast it has on the people around us, including ourselves. Dealing with our emotions is a skill. It's about listening to our emotions, not resisting them.

Emotions are meant to be felt through completely so we can figure out why we are feeling them. When we ignore them, we can't understand why and where they are coming from. If we can't understand them, we can't move past them into the state of habitual happiness we all deserve.

It's important that we feel through the emotion, telling ourselves, "I'm going to feel through this emotion until it's done" — even if it's painful or uncomfortable. Then later, we have to ask ourselves, "Why was I feeling this way?" Usually the reason is deeper than the surface event that caused the emotion. Seeing an emotion through could even be our surprising teacher, helping us to eliminate an insecurity that's holding us back.

So tell yourself the truth, feel your emotions and figure out why you're feeling them. They were made to help us grow, not to be kept in a bottle. This is especially true of the emotion of fear. Fear, as we discussed earlier, can be nothing more than comfort in disguise. But how can we know that we are staying in our comfort zones if we come up with excuses for why we didn't do the do?

Excuses are merely lies. "I didn't do it because I was tired. I didn't do it because it didn't make sense. I didn't do it because I was running late." These are all lies we tell ourselves to make ourselves feel better about not doing what we said we would do, or not following the internal nudge from within.

Just tell yourself the truth, which is that you didn't do something because you weren't disciplined enough, or because you were afraid. You know what? That's perfectly okay! We are allowed to mess up and still be working on discipline. (Discipline is a skill. Look at the resources section to learn how to develop it). We are allowed to feel fear, and we are all allowed to not act due to fear. First, we should forgive ourselves, because we can't control the past. Then it's important to realize that this doesn't make us any less of a person. Instead, it shows us an opportunity to grow. Hooray growth!

When we lie to ourselves about not doing things because of a lack of discipline or out of fear, we are not able to solve the problem, which is our excuses. Excuses from the past then lead to excuses for the future.

I was walking my dog on a walking trail one day. It was a hot summer day, and I usually walk without my shirt on to get my tan on. When I was walking, I saw someone sitting on a bench, clearly contemplating something. I then got the nudge from within: "Go sit next to him and strike up a conversation." Immediately the excuses starting pouring in. "He looks like he wants to be alone. What if he doesn't like dogs? I don't even have a shirt on, it'll be silly. He probably doesn't want to talk to me anyway. You know what, he's probably a serial killer.

Yep, I definitely made the right decision by moving on." I gave myself all these excuses because I didn't want to admit that I was actually afraid to do it. I was afraid of him rejecting me and not wanting to talk to me.

A few weeks later, I found myself in the exact same situation — same guy, just a different bench. The nudge from within struck again, and so did the excuses. This time, as I moved past him, I recognized that I was actually lying to myself, and that what I was experiencing was fear. "You know what, I am actually just afraid to go talk to him, and that's okay. I don't have to go back to try and talk to him now. Being afraid doesn't make me less of a person. It's just an opportunity to grow in the future."

Unfortunately, I never did see him again. He may have been an excellent person to have networked with. Maybe he wanted someone to bounce ideas off of. Or maybe he just needed a friend. I'll never know because I had initially lied to myself. When we recognize that we are afraid, it gives us the opportunity to be courageous the next time. When we lie to ourselves about being afraid, it leads us to hide in our comfort zones. Comfort zones can cause us to lie to people in different settings.

We sometimes lie to get out of invitations. "I'm sorry, I have this thing I really have to do, on that exact day, at that exact time! What a coincidink! But next time, for sure, count me in!" It's better just to say you don't want to go. If it's someone you don't like, maybe they'll invite you less often! If it's someone you do like, then why would you treat that person with such disrespect? Just tell them why you don't want to go, and tell them you are just being honest. If they have a problem with that, at least you're remaining authentic!

Then there is the context of relationships. Have you ever heard that communication is the key ingredient to every successful relationship? That is only half true: *honest* communication is the key ingredient to every successful relationship. It's being completely honest in everything you do, especially how certain things make you feel. It may be uncomfortable because there is vulnerability in things not working out. But if you don't tell the truth, things won't work out anyway; it will just blow up later on.

One day, one of my former girlfriends and I decided to become business partners. I was extremely excited to start a partnership with this lovely lady, who I believed would make a phenomenal team with me. We even pinky promised! Total business partners now.

One morning, I could tell she was very uncomfortable about something. I kept asking her what it was, but she kept saying, "I'm fine." Every guy knows "I'm fine" is code for "SOMETHING IS TERRIBLY WRONG! SOUND THE ALARMS! FIX THE PROBLEM NOW!" I knew that honest communication was the only way relationships truly succeed, so I kept bugging her. She eventually admitted that she didn't want to start a business with me—that she really belongs in corporate America. She's a genius at networking, so working for a large corporation naturally made sense at the time. It took me a while to process that, but eventually I was grateful she told me the truth. Otherwise, it would have forced her into something she is not, which kills a relationship every time.

Just because two people stay together in the end doesn't mean the relationship was successful. The relationship becomes successful when two people feel they are able to be completely themselves around each other. In other words, when both people are completely happy when they are around each other. Otherwise, what's the point of the relationship? If it doesn't bring you happiness, doesn't lead to more happiness, or doesn't prevent a decrease in happiness in the future, what's the point of anything?

Honest communication in our relationships begins with telling each other how we feel about certain things and situations, but we can do that without letting our emotions control the conversation. We can express our anger in a normal tone of voice. We can express our disappointment with a reason behind it. We can express how we feel without creating a full-blown, heated argument. Honest communication about our feelings always reveals why we are feeling the way we do, which always leads to solutions. It can be uncomfortable, but it's the only way a successful, happy relationship is possible. Honest communication is vital in really everything that we do.

Being yourself isn't possible without honesty. In moments where you aren't being honest, you aren't being yourself. The skill of honesty is about telling the truth in every moment, however we may feel in that moment. It's about correcting our lies when we do quickly indulge back into that habit of lying. The more quickly we admit we have lied, the less uncomfortable admitting the lie will be. Correcting the lie also instills the habit of being completely honest in the first place.

It can be uncomfortable to be honest in situations in which some people may take our honesty the wrong way. But we can be honest without being brutally honest. This isn't about sugar coating the truth; it's about being honest from a place of compassion and sincerity.

People really appreciate honesty. Yes, it may not feel great all the time, but it feels far better than when someone has found out you have lied. If you consistently tell people the truth, the ones who are meant to be in your life will stay. The people who aren't meant to be in your life will go. It's that simple. When you adopt the skill of authenticity, you're able to help serve the people you were meant to serve while also keeping your integrity and staying true to who you are.

CHAPTER THIRTEEN

See the Spider, Be the Spider

"If you give a man a fish, you feed him for a day. If you teach a man to fish, you feed him for a lifetime."

– Lao Tzu, Ancient Chinese Philosopher

Teaching is a skill, and like every skill, we can learn how to teach others. Parents know the value of teaching. They can tie a child's shoe every single time, or they can teach their child how to tie their own shoes and never have to tie them ever again. In the short run, doing things for others is a lot easier than teaching them. Tie the kid's shoe, and it's tied. But then you're the one who has to keep tying the shoe over and over again. In the long run, putting in the patience and effort to teach someone always benefits everyone. The child learns and can handle things independently, and the parent doesn't have to waste time always tying the shoe, hopefully learning patience along the way.

Patience is a requirement for learning new skills, but it's even more important for teaching new skills. When children fail and see frustration in a teacher or parent, they begin to fear failure. Then they see failure as something that causes frustration, not as something that helps you succeed in the future.

Failure is the only way we truly learn. If you miss a question on your homework, you keep learning to get it right on the test. You miss a shot in practice, you keep learning to make the shot in the game. You go bankrupt in your first business, you learn how to succeed in your next one —or maybe even the one after that.

When we fear failure, we become afraid of trying anything new. We become afraid to *learn* anything new. That's why doing the "do" becomes so important. The "do" usually wants us to try new things, despite the discomfort of possible failure.

Failure and rejection go hand and hand; we learn from rejection as much as we do from failure. Rejection allows us to realize that not everyone has to like us in order for us to love ourselves. We learn that we can fail in front of others and still keep our heads held high because we learned something. Failure always lifts us up to succeed in the future if we learn something from it. Please remember this the next time that internal nudge wants you to be vulnerable.

We can fear failure because of parental frustration, but we can also fear failure because of what other people might say when they hear or see we failed. A lot of that has to do with our education system, and how it has created such a competitive environment. But it's also because our education system unknowingly sets most students up for failure.

Classrooms today have from twenty to thirty students. Classes are taught as if all thirty students learn the same way or at the same pace. This creates an assumption that some kids are smart and some kids are dumb. Untrue as this is, some children actually grow up believing that they are stupid, when in fact we are all geniuses in our own unique way.

Our education system treats our brains as if they were cups, trying to fill up the cup with as much knowledge as possible. The children with the fewest holes in their cups (i.e., the ones who can retain the most knowledge) are more likely to be successful in the game of life. But life isn't a game of winners and losers, or of successes and failures. Life's a game of learners and the learned, the ones who improve and the ones who get worse. Having finished school, some people think that the process of learning is complete, and that there's no more to learn, or that they don't *have* to learn any more. They become the ones who think they know it all, the ones called "the learned."

"In times of change, learners will inherit the earth, while the learned find themselves beautifully equipped to deal with a world that no longer exists."

– Eric Hoffer, Philosopher

With the Information Age rapidly expanding everyone's knowledge and changing the world as we know it, staying the same means falling behind.

Learning and growing is how we improve our lives; otherwise, our lives will stay the same. Ask any personal growth enthusiast, and they will tell you that learning is one of the most fulfilling experiences we can encounter. The rewards we get from learning something new are indescribable. When our effort, patience and persistence through failure finally pay off, there's a sense of accomplishment that inspires us to learn and grow more.

Learning isn't something we should *have* to do; learning is something we should be excited that we *get* to do. When we try to fill children's brains with useless information, they start to hate learning (or they think they hate learning). They think they hate learning because they've been forced in school to study subjects they dislike or don't care about, or they've been tricked into believing they can't learn, when ironically our education system just doesn't understand how true learning works.

We have an education system that pours a bunch of useless knowledge into our heads to see who can memorize and who can't—and then calls that learning. There is a huge difference between understanding something and memorizing something. Understanding is achieved when knowledge becomes instinctive; memorizing is merely verbal repetition. Anyone can memorize the number system, but it takes an understanding to apply the number system to real mathematics. This is why mathematics is considered one of the hardest subjects to learn, because it requires more than just memorization.

Everyone can learn and understand math. Our education system teaches math through repetition. The attitude is, teach the fundamentals and then give the students an endless amount of problems to solve until they figure the rest out. The mentality is that the "smart" ones get it, and the rest are just "dumb." But understanding knowledge isn't like a cup we fill to see how much water we can retain. Understanding knowledge is more like a spider web we weave.

In the case of a real spider web, the spider first lets out a string of silk and swings it, hoping that it attaches to something. When it finally attaches the first string to something, it crawls down that strand of silk and begins to weave the web one step at a time, gradually building it as it moves along what it has already made. However, the spider can't build in an area that doesn't already have a strand of silk for it to crawl onto. It must build on existing strands to create and continue making the web. The way we understand knowledge is like the spider weaving its web.

Have you ever been studying something, struggling to understand it, when all of a sudden it just clicks? When you finally "get it," you wonder how you couldn't understand it in the first place. Learning that subject becomes more fluid from then on. It's because knowledge is like a spider web, and before it clicked, you were trying to build knowledge in an area that didn't have silk for you to build on.

If you're taking calculus, for instance, without having a solid foundation in algebra, you're unlikely to comprehend it. You may grasp some of it, but not everything that you will need to be "successful" in the class. It's not that you couldn't fully understand calculus or algebra; it's that you weren't able to connect the new knowledge with what you already knew.

If you are sick one day and miss a fundamental building block of algebra, you most likely would have to learn that material on your own at home, in which case you may not be able to connect what you are learning to the web of what you already knew. Or maybe you didn't pay attention in class one day, because you find algebra boring, or there were problems at home or with bullying at school, or algebra was your last class of the day and you were tired, or the teacher may have been inadequate. There are an infinite number of reasons why you might not have been able to connect the web of knowledge. It's not that you couldn't learn that subject, or that you're stupid; it's just because you missed a building block, which prohibited you from connecting what you had already learned with what you are learning now. This would then affect learning in all related subject areas.

Spider webs are just different patterns of lines that extend in different directions. Each line can be likened to a different area of study. Some subject areas meet and touch at different spots in the web of knowledge. In order to fully understand physics, you have to understand some aspects of mathematics. Since science and math are closely related, we sometimes conclude that some people are "math and science people" and others are not, when the truth is that some of us may have just missed a fundamental building block that prevented us from learning anything else in those subjects.

Everyone is a genius who can learn anything. Sure, some of us may have a harder time learning particular subjects. It may take us more effort and patience than it would someone else, but that's because we all have unique talents, and our effort and patience are more valuably used for those different skills.

If you aren't interested in math, that's fine! Find out what you are interested in, or what you can understand quickly, and go after it! The web of knowledge can be used to learn anything, not just school subjects.

Learning new knowledge is a series of building connections from knowledge we have previously learned, not a series of random facts that we try to force into our memories. You can't put the roof on a building right after you've finished the foundation. There's a process you have to complete before you can get to the next step.

If you're a teacher, coach, mentor, trainer, role model, parent or sibling, learning the skill of teaching is crucial. Teaching begins with meeting the student where they are. It's about figuring out where their web of knowledge ends and helping them build from there. The best way to ensure someone gets what you are teaching is by using analogies with what they already understand.

If you're teaching a child math, if you can somehow relate a new math concept to something they already understand, they are more likely to comprehend it. If they like video games, relate the math concepts to a video game they play. When you relate new knowledge to something they are already interested in and understand, the better you can teach them the new idea. This works for anyone — kids and adults.

So then teaching is not a procedure we repeat until the student pretends to understand it by repeating it back at us. Instead, teaching is a flexible plan specifically tailored to a student's need. If it's a mere procedure, teachers may try to teach students something they are not ready to understand. Repetition is of course the key to mastering a new skill, but repetition without understanding is just continually repeating what we do not know.

Repetition may work with students eventually, because if you were to repeat something often enough they inevitably will understand it. But with repetition to understand something, the question isn't a matter of if they will ever learn it or not; the question is, how long will it take?

Sometimes even a full school year isn't enough time to repeatedly teach something so that a student will comprehend it. School systems today do not teach one subject in a school year. They teach multiple "mini" subjects in a school year — sometimes called units, and units do not last long enough for most students to fully grasp the concepts they are learning. The problem is, that information will be needed to be able to learn the next unit.

Think of these building blocks like a dial with numbers one through infinity. If a student is on dial number seven and you try to teach them information that's on dial number nine, they probably won't understand it. You have to teach them the dial number eight information first for them to move up a notch on the dial. The student's current dial number is called their "awareness" level, or where they're at on the web of knowledge.

Asking questions allows you to get further insight into where a person is on the web of knowledge. The answers to those questions reveal what they know and can understand. Remember, the simple fact that someone doesn't know something does not mean they are stupid. It just means no one has taught them that information yet. Just because someone doesn't seem to understand something now doesn't mean they never will. It just means they are missing some strand of silk on the web related to that idea, concept or subject. Keep digging deeper to find the missing link between what the student already knows and what you are trying to teach them. That is, of course, only if they want to learn what it is you have to teach.

I have realized that you can't teach people who don't want to be taught, or whose minds are closed off to what you are teaching. It's like trying to force change on someone who doesn't want to change. Teaching people your way of thinking without their asking for it is wasted effort. It just leads to disappointment and sometimes results in arguments. This doesn't mean you shouldn't spread your ideas. It just means you shouldn't force your ideas onto others. The people who listen to you are the ones whose web you can further build upon. If you try to teach someone who has closed off their web to you, i.e., has a closed mind to the subject you are teaching, your effort will always be wasted.

At the end of the day, teaching is about helping other people. It's how we spread our knowledge, gathered through our experiences, to others. Everyone can teach at least one thing to someone else. Anyone over the age of probably five has had at least one experience that you or I haven't had. If someone else has had an experience we haven't had, we can learn something new from them. Just make sure what you're learning—and for that matter, teaching—has the potential to improve your life rather than to make you worry about something you can't control.

When you are able to teach more people, you are able to learn more yourself. Some people may even have a different perspective on what you are teaching, which can make you think about things differently.

When teaching, we should always encourage people to learn the things they want to learn, so that they will enjoy learning. People only learn what they want to learn! It sounds obvious, but we sometimes force subjects on people that they don't enjoy — especially in school. This doesn't mean that we shouldn't teach children basic mathematics or language skills; rather it means we don't have to force them into advanced studies that they will most likely never use in the real world. If each student has a different web of knowledge, how can a traditional classroom setting help all students learn effectively? The truth is, they can't. So instead of understanding that part of the education system is broken, some students falsely believe that they can't learn. And if they believe they can't learn, they obviously won't enjoy learning.

Taking away someone's joy in learning is one of the worst things we can do to a person. Without the joy of learning, people don't want to learn. When they don't want to learn, they stay the same. In staying the same, they are dooming themselves in a world that is constantly changing and improving. As they stay the same, the world keeps moving, and they get left behind.

One of the best things you can teach anyone is the art of being themselves. When you teach people how to be themselves, you're really teaching them how to be happy. In order to teach people to be themselves, you have to be able to give them the greatest gift that anyone can receive.

CHAPTER FOURTEEN

The Greatest Gift

"I suffer whenever I see that common sight of a parent or senior imposing his opinion and way of thinking and being on a young soul to which they are totally unfit. Cannot we let people be themselves, and enjoy life in their own way? You are trying to make that man another you. One's enough."

– Ralph Waldo Emerson, Philosopher

Free will, or the power to choose, is the greatest gift that we can give someone. In other words, the freedom to be *themselves*. Everyone has free will, but not everyone seems to exercise it. Like everything else in life, choosing is a skill. Most people feel like they don't have a choice. They feel obligated by the pressures of the outside world to do what other people want for them. This can be especially true in the case of our parents.

When I was on my "Lone Wolf" journey, I decided to volunteer at a camp in August. Kate's Club, which is a phenomenal non-profit organization that helps children through grief of a loved one, offers a camp twice a year. It is designed to let the children have as much fun as possible, while also engaging in activities that allow them to understand how to deal with grief in a healthy way, instead of suppressing it. I was one of the supervisors for the eight- and nine-year-old boys. This was really my first time ever dealing with children as a young adult.

Everything at the camp obviously revolved around the children, so my thinking had to be about how to behave in front of them (which can be difficult if you aren't used to it). Instead of thinking about what was best for me, I had to think about what was best for the children: how to keep them safe, how they should or shouldn't interact with each other, and the like. I had to alter my behavior around them. It wasn't a matter of me trying to act like something I wasn't, but rather expanding my behavior to reflect who I am in a different context, a context that's more appropriate to children.

I learned several things during this experience. One was to never, ever judge a parent. Raising children is a full-time job. In addition, parents also have to make money and deal with the rest of life. So in this book, I'm not judging parents, but instead offering a new way of thinking. We all have our own definitions of being ourselves and what success looks like. When you're a parent or a primary caretaker, you know that your job is to teach and raise your children to be the best people they can be, so it becomes reasonable for a parent or guardian to transplant their beliefs and ideals to the way they think the child should act. Of course, this is necessary — up to a certain age.

When children become mature enough to make their own decisions, we should let them. The job of a parent is not to mold their child into what the parent wants them to be. The job of parents is to give their children the tools to be able to mold themselves.

There is one simple caveat to all of this: I am not yet a parent, so I have no idea what it's actually like to raise a child. My only experience in raising children is three days at camp, and obviously that is a very limited amount of time to learn. But I do have the perspective of being a child to a parent. I think that when some people become parents, they sometimes forget their own experiences as a child, or how the pressure of being what their parents wanted them to be affected them. Instead, they focus on how their parents raised them. They either follow the way their parents raised them, because that's what they were taught, or they do the complete opposite if they didn't like how they were raised. But if parents stick to the fundamental concept of expecting their children to be something they want them to be, how can their children grow up to be happy? They're living the parent's ideal life, not their own. I'm not saying all parents do this, but some definitely do.

Happiness comes from loving ourselves, not from pleasing other people so that they love us. That means that if we want the people we love to be happy, we have to be able to encourage them to be themselves so that they can love themselves, even if they decide to do or be something that we do not want for them.

A great example of this is the movie *Dead Poets Society.* It's about a group of teenagers who attend an elite prep school called Welton Academy. One of the characters, Neil Perry, constantly exhibits the fear of losing the approval of his father. His father wants him to go to an Ivy League school so he can then go to medical school to become a doctor. While at the academy, Neil discovers his love for acting by participating in the school play. He tries to keep his father unaware of his love for acting because he knows his father will make him quit acting to focus on his studies. His father eventually finds out and tells him to quit the play immediately. After his dad sees Neil act in the play, he decides to send Neil to military school to end this "foolishness" once and for all. Neil begs his dad to let him stay and continue to act on the side while he still works on his studies. His father won't hear of it, but instead forces his idea of success onto Neil. With no apparent way around the pressure to be someone he is not, Neil takes his father's revolver, and kills himself.

Suicide is devastating. When you hear about someone committing suicide, it leads to so many questions. Why? Could I have done something? Should I have reached out more? Could this have been prevented? Suicide happens from a deep depression, a sense of sadness that feels like there is no hope, that the only escape is to just end the emotional pain. Every situation is different, but I think the main cause of suicide is the feeling of living a life you were not meant to live, and the sense that you never will. I know, because I have had thoughts of ending it all.

I have never attempted suicide, but I used to think about what it would be like to no longer be living. In times of deep sadness, when I felt like nothing would ever get better, this thought would constantly cross my mind. The sadness was really a feeling of living a life that wasn't meant for me, causing me to hate myself instead of loving myself. It felt as if I didn't have a choice to do what I wanted in my life, but in fact I had just allowed other people's opinions to dictate my choices for me.

This feeling that there is no chance of being ourselves doesn't always come from our parents. It can come from anywhere, especially from the pressure's of being successful society tends to throw on us. For me, it came from a fear of other people's opinions — that my choices would be judged negatively. It came from doubts and fears that I would never be good enough to achieve what I wanted in life. Those doubts and fears weren't really mine, but rather, the voices in my head of other people who told me, "You can't. It's not possible."

If you know someone who has committed suicide — even if it was someone close to you — please know it was absolutely not your fault. They made the choice of death over reaching out. All you can do is try to heal from it, and maybe give other people the greatest gift they can receive.

The greatest gift you can give people is the freedom to be themselves. If you want to do more than that, *encourage* them to be themselves. When you judge someone as being different than you, or for not living life the way you want them to, you aren't giving them the freedom to be themselves.

Have you ever felt like you've been judged? Of course you have; we all have. The judgment is written all over their body language, their tone of voice, and their facial expressions. Perhaps we even hear them talking behind our backs. It can be obvious when someone passes judgment on us. It's almost as if they purposely do a bad job of hiding their judgments. "I'm secretly judging you, but also letting you know that I am." Sometimes they even judge us to our faces.

How does it feel to be judged? Do you enjoy it? Does it encourage you to continue to be yourself? What if you've ever judged others? Are you happy judging others? I'm assuming the answer is probably no.

Judging others is also making comparisons with others. It's us evaluating how they are behaving. It's saying, "I don't approve of their behavior. They should be acting the way I want them to. I think I am better than they are, and I think they should know it."

Sometimes we even judge people for things they have done in the past. When we criticize or judge someone for past actions, we create an environment that assumes people can't change. You often see this in the media. Someone has an excellent reputation, and they are doing all the right things in their present-day life. Then someone else finds something they posted on social media, or about something they did years ago, and people act as if the ones they are judging did it yesterday. People can change. Let's focus on the good they are doing in the present instead of judging them for something they did in the past.

Judging others is really ignorance. Ignorance seems like such a bad word, almost as if it means being stupid. But it doesn't mean that someone is stupid; it means they haven't been taught something. It really just means lacking information or knowledge. We are all ignorant of something, but judging others ignores the fact that everyone else has been raised differently than we were. It's ignorant of the fact that because people were raised differently, they were taught to speak and act differently in different situations. It disregards the fact that people can change, and that through their mistakes and failures they are able to grow, learn and become more than they once were. Instead of judging, let's try observing. "I observe that their behavior is not the way I would act in this scenario, but the person I am observing obviously has been taught differently. Their behavior is a reflection of who they are, not who I am. It is completely okay for them to express who they are." And: "I observe that what they did in the past was a reflection of who they once were and not who they are now. Through their mistakes, they have learned valuable lessons that have clearly moved them in a positive direction." Observing comes from a place of compassion. Judging comes from a place of resentment.

"The ability to observe without evaluating is the highest form of intelligence."

– Jiddu Krishnamurti, Indian Philosopher

Unfortunately, I still catch myself judging people sometimes too, but it's something that takes patience and effort to stop doing. Observing rather than judging can be a difficult skill to learn, but we *all* can learn it. It's a mental skill, so it begins with an awareness that we are judging someone, and then shifting our thinking to observation and compassion.

Judgments are really just a cousin of expectations. Without even thinking about it, we all have expectations about how other people should act in certain situations, which causes our judgments. We also have expectations about what people should know how to do, or shouldn't do. But not everyone has been taught the same skills and lessons that we have.

When I was a kid growing up, I was very selfish with how I wanted things to happen. I would ask my parents to do things in a way that inconvenienced everyone else, but would help me get what I wanted. Every time I would ask my parents to do something that seemed selfish in their eyes, their usual response was, "Well, the world doesn't revolve around Jamie!" Nothing during my entire childhood made me angrier than when my parents would say this to me, mainly because I had no idea that my requests were selfish. I knew the world didn't revolve around me, but I didn't have the skill set needed to think about how my requests affected other people. No one had taught me those skills, they just expected me to know how to do it. And you know what? No one had taught my parents that this was a skill that needed to be taught to their children.

We only know what we have been taught to know! We all learn things in different situations, whether that's being taught by other people or through our own experiences. But we all start with a blank canvas, so it's impossible to know something if no one has taught us (and that includes our own self-study).

We all seem to have expectations. When we give someone a present, we expect them to be grateful or to like it. When we give someone a compliment, we expect them to accept it, and perhaps even smile. But what happens when we have expectations that aren't met? Disappointment. Continuous disappointment leads to resentment.

Sometimes we expect people not to do things, so we tell ourselves the outcome before they even do it. "If Johnny goes golfing again today, I'm going to be really upset." "If my girlfriend goes to that party tonight, I'm going to be mad." "If Billy plays video games all day, I'm going to get very angry." The problem with these statements, or with expectations in general, is that your happiness becomes conditional on the actions of others. You then are no longer in control of your happiness; it is out of your hands. Habitual happiness comes from *our* choices. We can choose to be happy by focusing on ourselves and the things we can control, or we can choose to base our happiness on the actions of others. Happiness is guaranteed with the former choice. It's a risk with the latter.

In relationships, we sometimes expect to be able to change our friends, family, and especially our lovers into the people we want them to be. We sometimes even marry people expecting them to change because we are now married. The truth is that there is only one person in the entire universe you can change, and that is yourself.

Since college, I have always wanted to somehow change the world, to make it a better place than it was before. I thought in order to change the world, I had to change other people. Instead of focusing on changing myself, I focused on changing others.

My former fiancée always wanted to be a mother to a happy family. I wanted to be an entrepreneur, and I wanted my partner to be an entrepreneur with me. So, I tried to make her one to fit into what I wanted, instead of letting her be who she wanted to be. I tried to form a lucrative business that would put me into the spotlight to "change" other people and would allow her to use her natural gifts as well. She is an absolute genius at baking. People are usually good at either making things taste good or making them look pretty. She could do both. So I came up with the idea of starting a marijuana-baking business. The green rush was the new gold rush, and baking was our ticket in.

So we moved to a state with legalized marijuana. We even bought a nice house out there. She was happy with the house, and I was happy to get started on the business, which we called Trippy Treats. It turns out that there are a lot of regulations to enter the marijuana industry, and you need thousands, if not millions, of dollars to get started. (I learned the value of research). She was just happy to have a house to be able to start a family within the distant future, but I was miserable. Instead of being grateful for all that we had, I focused on how things weren't going the way I expected them to. I convinced her that we should sell the house and move back to our home state. Without even thinking about what she wanted, I pushed my entrepreneurial agenda on her and took away her beloved house, thinking that moving back home would make me happy. Surprise! It didn't.

Several months later, we were sitting on the couch watching a YouTube video my mom had sent me. It was an interview with Lisa Nichols by Tom Bilyeu. In the interview, Lisa said, "The doorway is for you to fit through. You're trying to carry everybody else through because you're trying to be rescue 911, and you have to rescue you first." We looked at each other, knowing why neither of us were happy. I was trying to lead her through my doorway to success, and she was trying to lead me through hers.

We all have different definitions of success and paths to it. Dragging others through our doorways kills the relationship we have with them. Relationships are a series of compromises, but don't compromise who you are for the relationship. Otherwise, you will always be unhappy because you aren't being who you truly are, who you were meant to be.

We can't change other people, and if we do, it's by force and not from their own free will. All we can do is give people the tools to be able to change themselves and keep them accountable for their behavior when they tell us they want to change. My goal is no longer to change anyone, but to give them the tools to help them change themselves into who they want to be—who they truly are. Forcing change leads to resentment. Helping change leads to happiness.

We can't love ourselves if we aren't being ourselves. If someone is forcing us to be someone we are not with their apparent judgments and disapproval, or threatens to end the relationship if we don't change into who they want us to be, or if we fall into their manipulative game, we cannot love ourselves because we are not being ourselves. And if we can't love ourselves, we can't love the person who is forcing the change on us.

The same is true in reverse. If we force someone to be something they are not, they will end up resenting us because they hate who they have become for us. Why have our happiness be conditional on what others do or don't do? Let's let other people be who they were meant to be without trying to force them to be the people we want them to be.

The reason there is so much global hatred isn't because of cultural differences; it's because of the way we view cultural differences. Instead of respecting each other's cultures, we expect people to assimilate to our own. We can respect each other's beliefs without trying to change them, but it's as if there are boxes that society tries to place us all in. Religions have their boxes that they try and fit their followers into. Political parties have their boxes. The education system has boxes that they try to force students into. The way society views money as success is its own box. The way society views how women should act or even look is a box. There's even a box for the way celebrities should act, and anything they do outside of that box makes it into headline news. We are all taught that there's a certain box we must fit into, and to act outside that box is disrespectful to the people forcing us into the box. In reality, acting within a box that doesn't fit who we are is disrespectful to *ourselves*. We aren't meant to fit into boxes with limitations. We are meant to be limitless, to be able to change the world—in a way that is big or small.

If you want to change the world, change the only person you can: yourself. Changing yourself is a never-ending process. It's the most rewarding, limitless experience you can possibly imagine. And in the midst of change, the best thing you can do is help others.

Always remember that you can't really change anyone. All you can do is help by giving them the tools to change themselves. The first step in fostering change is to remind people that they can change. Let them know that the boxes aren't real, that they are simply figments of our imaginations. The freedom to be themselves is the greatest gift we can give someone. Our greatest present doesn't come in a box. It comes through words that say, "I love you for who you are." After all, love is what we are all really searching for.

CHAPTER FIFTEEN

My Message to You

"Love Everyone Always"

Those three simple words contain my message to you. When you have negative thoughts about others, when you hold resentments toward them, or when you focus on people in the world with hatred for things you cannot control, how do you feel? Are you peaceful and happy? Or are you angry and fearful? You know the latter is true.

Can you imagine what it would feel like to Love Everyone Always? Do you think you could ever get angry or upset if there was nothing but love in your heart?

Let's take the analogy of squeezing a lemon. If you squeeze a lemon, what comes out of it? Of course, lemon juice comes out. There is no chance of apple juice or grape juice coming out when you squeeze a lemon. Why? Because lemon juice is what's inside. So if we extend the metaphor of a lemon to us as humans, what comes out of us must be what's inside. It doesn't matter if our brother squeezes us, or our arch-nemesis, or the guy who cut us off in traffic. If anger, fear, or resentment comes out of us, it is only because that's what's inside.

Loving Everyone Always is the source of permanent happiness. When we allow what other people do or say to affect our mood, we are still putting our happiness in their hands, whether what they do or say is right or wrong. When we get angry at what someone says about us, what we are really saying is, "What they think of me is more important than what I think of myself." Our emotions come from the inside; no one can make us feel a certain way unless we let them. We must understand that just because someone says something, that alone doesn't make it true—it will only be true if *we* believe it. It is more a reflection of them than it is of us.

Loving Everyone Always is the step that follows learning to love yourself, surrounding yourself with the right people, and developing the skills that put you into a purposeful, fulfilling life. That's where you turn your habitual happiness into everlasting happiness, a happiness that can't be altered from without and is cemented from within.

How do you Love Everyone Always? It sounds like a fairy tale or something that is reserved for the divine. But the truth is that it's possible for *everyone* to achieve. Have I achieved this yet? No, but I work on it daily. Will I get there? I intend to, but even if I don't, I believe it's worth striving for.

Since trying to Love Everyone Always, I have noticed that my attention is focused more on the good in the world than on the bad. Every moment spent thinking positively is happier than any moment spent thinking negatively. Every moment of every day adds up to our entire life. Every moment spent thinking positively and loving makes the outcome of our life that much more positive and loving.

If you think it's impossible to Love Everyone Always, why not try anyway? Like everything else in life, Loving Everyone Always is a skill we all can learn. The more we practice it, the better we get and the more meaningful our lives become to the people we leave behind. We not only find out for ourselves that it's worth it, but we also teach the people we will eventually leave behind that it's worth it. That's how we truly start to make the world a better place than before we arrived.

So how can we start to cultivate the skill of Loving Everyone Always? First, let's talk about what love is not. Love is not a competition, nor is it conditional. "I love you more! No, I love you more! I love you more than she does! I'll only love you if you do this for me. I'll only love you if you act this way. I'll only love you if you be the person I want you to be." These common misconceptions about love describe attachment, not love. Attachment is fear disguised as love. It's the fear that you're going to lose that person. Attachment says, "If I love them more, they have to stay with me." It says, "I know they want my love, so I'll manipulate their fear of losing it to get what I want from them." Attachment says, "My life isn't worth living if that one person isn't in it." Or worse, attachment says, "I hate them now that they are no longer with me."

When most people think of love, they think of their spouses, children and other family members, or even their pets. However, there is a huge difference between loving someone and wanting to be around someone. The examples above are of the people you want to be around, to the point where it is very easy to love them. And you do love them. You enjoy their company and hopefully they enjoy yours.

But you can love someone and not want to be around them. True, unconditional love for someone is simply wishing them well—to wish that they are happy or on their way to becoming happy. That can be from a distance, but it's this sense of peace that acknowledges that everyone is here to learn, do and be something. Everyone is going through something in their lives, big or small. Consequently, we sometimes allow outside pressures to dictate how we act around each other. But the core of our very being is love for everyone. We are born hard-wired to love. We are then taught to hate.

Hate is learned. Love is what is natural. We all share 99.9% of the same DNA. The 0.1% makes us all unique. The 99.9% makes us all brothers and sisters.

Loving Everyone Always is not easy. If it were easy, everyone would do it. It is particularly difficult when someone makes you angry, especially if it's a stranger. It's not easy when someone wrongs you. It's not easy when someone steals from you. It's not easy when someone sends hate in your direction, especially when it's for no other reason than your just being different from them. So how can we Love Everyone Always? Through the skills of forgiveness, empathy and compassion.

Forgiving yourself is vital for your happiness, but it's equally vital to forgive others as well. When you hold a grudge against someone, are you actually hurting them? Do your negative thoughts about them make them unhappy? Or do they just make *you* unhappy?

Forgiveness of others isn't for them, it's for us. It's for us to recognize that what they did is a reflection of who they are, not of who we are. When we allow them to make us angry for something they did in the past, we're letting them win by taking away our present happiness. We don't have to be in the presence of someone to forgive them, but we do have to be able to let them enter our mind without having feelings of hatred, resentment or anger. Forgiveness is a mental skill. It's acknowledging when we feel emotions of resentment toward ourselves or someone else from our past and trying to shift that into loving ourselves or wishing them well. It's not always easy, but it is always worth it, and it does get easier each time you do it.

Another way to forgive people from your past, and also to observe rather than judge, is through empathy. Empathy is the ability to put yourself in other people's shoes. Given the situation at hand with the information they know, and given what you know about that person regarding how they may have been raised to believe or think, would you have acted the same way in that situation? We all grow up with different beliefs and in different environments that mold who we are. How we act is a byproduct of who we are — what we believe. When you are able to feel empathy for another, you are then able to approach the situation with compassion.

If you google the definition of compassion at the time this book is being published, you will find the worst meaning of a word I have ever found. It states that compassion is "sympathetic pity and concern for the sufferings or misfortunes of others." No wonder no one feels compassion! Do you like to give sympathetic pity to people? Do you like to receive sympathetic pity from other people?

Compassion is simply understanding without justifying. Compassion is the ability to understand that everyone was born to love and then taught to hate. The hate and anger within that person is something you can be grateful you weren't raised with or have learned to turn into love and peace. It's saying, "I am grateful for who I am and what I've learned, and I understand that this other person is on a path where he or she must learn these things too." However, it is not justifying their behavior or beliefs. Understanding and justifying are completely different, despite the fact that some people may think they are not, which is why compassion can get misunderstood.

Understanding is to know where something comes from; justifying it would be to approve of it as acceptable. You can understand where it comes from, love that person, wish them well to learn love and peace, and still denounce their behavior and want justice for their actions.

When people have hatred towards others that is based on how someone looks, who someone is attracted to, or anything else that is out of people's control, I have compassion for the fact that the hater must be hurting deep down. I have compassion for the fact that they experience hate and anger for anyone they see as different from them. Can you imagine walking down the street and enjoying the day, and all of a sudden you're full of hatred for no other reason than how someone else looks? And then to act in a way that is cancerous to society? I have compassion for people who do that — I understand how they got to those beliefs and hope they can find happiness — but I would never accept their behavior and allow them to keep acting that way. The greatest gift you can give someone is the freedom to be themselves, but having prejudice toward others is not natural. It's the byproduct of other people's beliefs imposed on them by ego and insecurities. Giving them the freedom to be themselves, their true selves, is to help teach them that love is what is natural and hate is what is evil. Giving them the freedom to be themselves is to wish them well to find love in their hearts as opposed to the hate they are currently experiencing. It's to be able to transform their hatred into its counterpart: love.

Loving Everyone Always requires many skills. It takes learning compassion, empathy, forgiveness, open-mindedness and the ability to wish someone well even when they are sending you hate. But the benefits of Loving Everyone Always are a state of blissful peace almost beyond imagining. It launches us into a state of permanent happiness to the point where it is impossible to feel anything else. It's not about being perfect at it, it's about gradually building those skills through patience and effort. It's being aware of our thinking. It's realizing when we are feeling anger or thinking hateful thoughts towards someone, and then shifting our intention to compassion, empathy, forgiveness and wishing them well.

In everyday life, you can learn it when a reckless driver cuts you off, or in the times you notice that you feel ill will toward someone else. Every time you become aware and change your thoughts to be positive and loving, you have won. You have kept your peace and happiness by not letting others have the power to take it away from you.

If you want to help change the world to one of happiness, peace and love, start with yourself. Start with the man or woman in the mirror. Start cultivating love for yourself, and then for everyone else. It may take some time, but it's worth any time that can possibly go by. It is how we make the world a better place than it once was.

The biggest enemy we face as the human race is hate for one another, and there is only one way we can eliminate hate: transform it into love.

"Darkness cannot drive out darkness; only light can do that.
Hate cannot drive out hate; only love can do that."

– Martin Luther King, Jr., Civil Rights Leader and Visionary

CHAPTER SIXTEEN

The End to Your Beginning

"To be, or not to be. That is the question."

– William Shakespeare, British poet

Life is an infinite series of choices that reduce to two underlying decisions: to be yourself or to not be yourself. If you've heard the quote above from Shakespeare's play, *Hamlet*, you probably know it is spoken by Prince Hamlet as he is contemplating suicide. In a sense, making decisions that do not represent who you truly are — making the choice not to be yourself — is a form of suicide. It's killing the version of the life you were meant to live.

We all have a vision of the life we want to live, a dream we cling to. It's the picture in our minds that we find ourselves day-dreaming about, when we aren't lost in the busyness of outside stresses. It's like that dream, that vision of what our lives could be like, is calling out to us by name. It's drawing us toward it, maybe even teasing us about the life we could be living. And yet, most of us choose not to pursue it.

You can live that dream life. All you need is the courage to choose to do so. The first step toward your dream life is clarity. It's being clear about what it is that you actually want to do with your life. Who is it that you want to be? What is it that you want to accomplish? What in this world would you like to change, and who do you need to become to affect that change? All you have to do is shed the negative beliefs about yourself that aren't actually yours and cultivate the beliefs that your true self has waiting for you.

If you don't know the answers to these questions yet, don't give up until you find them! Experiment, get outside your comfort zone, and go after the life you truly want, not the life you think you can have. The only thing stopping you from living your ideal life is the belief that you can't, so get imaginative, get creative, and get excited. The moment you get excited about a life you can live is the moment you start moving toward it. All it takes is turning your doubts and fears into faith and excitement.

When that purpose, or your dream, comes to your mind, open your mind to the belief that you will achieve it. Keep an open mind to all the different people, and their knowledge, that may help you achieve your dreams. But also remember to keep your mind closed to all the voices that tell you that you can't.

Most people can only see things from their own point of view. They lack the skill set needed to put themselves in your shoes, to be able to see your vision, your dreams and your goals. They tell you that you can't because they can't imagine themselves being able to achieve that same feat. The only person who needs to know that you can do it is *you*. After all, other people aren't the ones who are going to get it done; you are.

The reason most people don't go after their dreams is the fear of failure. But when you're old and gray, which do you think you will regret more: trying and failing, or not having tried at all?

So try, go for it, and live your life knowing that you did everything you could to make your dreams come true. The only way your dreams will come true is by being yourself—your true self. If you haven't already guessed it, what I mean by your true self is what some people call your "higher self."

When we say "higher self," it makes us think it's something we have to attain, that it's higher than we already are, but that is simply not true. It's not something you have to achieve; it's something you already are. It's your true self, the one who loves you just the way you are. Your true self has always been there. It's been buried under the false beliefs society and other people gave you, beliefs that said, "You're not good enough." The truth is that you are more than good enough. You are everything you will ever need. So nurture your true self, the inner child that wants to laugh loud, smile broadly and play big. The only way to nurture that inner child is to recognize that the child is there.

We all have our goofy quirks that make us feel like children again. But as kids, we're told to stop behaving foolishly and to behave in a certain way, to quit daydreaming and pay attention in class, to quit fooling ourselves about what we can do with our lives and settle for what is given to us. So instead of being our true selves, we settle for what society wants us to be. We settle for what society says we should be. We settle for what society has told us we can be. But settling leads to unhappiness, and unhappiness leads to a life not worth living. In a world of unhappiness, show people what it's like to be happy. Show them how to be happy. Show them how to be themselves.

Happiness comes from a feeling of love. Habitual happiness comes from loving yourself. Permanent happiness is always loving yourself and everyone who comes your way. When you feel that happiness from within, that feeling of an inner child who laughs and smiles at everything, ask yourself, why am I happy right now? What you'll find is that you are simply being yourself, without the need for the approval of others.

They say you're only one thought away from a completely different life. I would counter that a thought isn't strong enough. You are only one *belief* away from a completely different life — the belief that who you are is made to perfection — imperfections and all. Your true self loves you, so love it back and create the life you were always meant to live.

The reason you do *everything* matters. Is it for others' approval, or are you doing it for *your* approval? Are you doing it to serve your ego, so that the world likes you? Or are you doing it to serve others, so that you may love the world? The choices you make are either out of love for yourself, or out of fear of the lack of approval of others. Every choice is to be yourself or to not be yourself. The choice is either happiness or unhappiness. If you continually choose happiness — choosing a life of self-love — then you will never go back to where you were before, because once you have experienced a life of self-love, you will never allow yourself to experience anything different. You may slip here and there, but those choices will only serve to remind you that happiness is the only life worth living.

Your journey begins every moment of every day, because you have the ability to choose your thoughts, words, and actions in every moment. And in so choosing, you are creating your life. So choose wisely.

"Don't ask what the world needs. Ask what makes you come alive, and go do it. Because what the world needs is people who have come alive."

– Howard Thurman, Civil Rights Leader and Author

Namaste.

RESOURCES

RESOURCE 1

Skills to Learn

"Once you stop learning, you start dying."

- Albert Einstein, Genius

Here is a list of skills I consider to be very important. However, just because I think they're important doesn't necessarily mean that you do. So pick and choose the skills you want to learn! With each skill, you will find ways to help learn and build upon those skills.

Health Skills: The skills for physical happiness.

At the time of this book's publication, I am a certified Personal Trainer and Nutritionist, so some of these health tips are not just from my own experiences, but from what I have been taught as well. Even if you think you're as healthy as can be, you may learn something.

If someone says they aren't happy, the first thing I'll ask them is, do you exercise? Do you have good eating habits? Do you get enough sleep? These are just the basics, but they are required for us to experience habitual physical happiness. These are all choices we make, to do or not to do.

Some people like to use the excuse of "not having enough time" to exercise, cook, or even to get plenty of sleep. Everyone has exactly the same amount of time each day. We all make time for what we prioritize. If you want to make happiness your priority, then feeling physically "happy" is a requirement. Good health is required for us to be physically happy, so I recommend trying to put some of these tips and strategies to use.

Nutrition:

When I began working on my confidence again at the beginning of last year, I resumed doing P90X. I worked out every day for over an hour for forty-two days straight. The result? I lost less than five pounds. That's because I didn't change any of my eating habits.

When people think of food for health, they immediately think of food as energy. Food is so much more than just energy. It is actually information. The food you eat tells your body how to behave. Release more of this hormone; release less of that hormone. Store this as fat, burn that for energy. Food tells your body what to do, whether you realize it or not.

When most people think of good nutrition, they think of diets. People go crazy for the latest diet fad and say it's the best diet there is. "Go on paleo! No, try keto! Do intermittent fasting! Make sure you eat five meals a day! You have to eliminate carbs! The carb monster is going for your belly!" The truth is that no one diet is best for everyone. There is only the diet that's best for you!

The best diet for you is one that you'll follow consistently, one that is aligned with your current lifestyle. You could even call it a lifestyle change instead of a diet, because the goal isn't to go on it, lose weight and then gain the weight back by falling into old eating patterns. The goal is to stay permanently healthy.

If you are on a diet that you can't follow, how do you think you will feel if you quit? Not good, not good at all. Make sure you give yourself a fighting chance, and tailor your new lifestyle changes to goals you can achieve!

Although every diet is different, most have similarities, which is why they actually work. Here are some eating strategies that will benefit you if you decide to embark on a new health journey:

- Drink lots of water
- Eat as few processed foods as possible
- Substitute white carbs for whole wheat, brown rice, or quinoa
- Stop eating two to three hours before bedtime
- Cook as many of your own meals as you can
- Be mindful of your eating habits
- Put your fork or spoon down after every bite
- Chew slowly and mindfully
- Listen when your body tells you to stop eating at every meal
- Stop counting calories

Drinking lots of water has numerous health benefits. It keeps you energized, improves satiation (or the feeling of fullness) and, obviously, your body craves water. Sometimes when you feel hungry, it's actually your body telling you that you're thirsty. Drinking lots of water also makes your skin elastic. So, when you start to lose weight, your skin is better prepared to adapt to your new body tone, and you'll have much less excess skin—which can be a concern for some people if they lose too much weight too fast. Most nutritionists recommend half your body weight in ounces of water a day. So if you weigh two hundred pounds, drink at least one hundred ounces of water a day.

Eating highly processed foods is the main reason people are so overweight. Such foods delay satiation, which means they prevent you from feeling full even though you are. They also light up pleasure sensors in the brain. Have you ever ordered something that tasted really bland but kept eating it anyway, even to the point of feeling too full? That's because highly processed foods make your brain want more, even if it doesn't taste all that good.

One way to avoid highly processed foods is to cook more often! People think of cooking as a time-consuming task that they don't have the luxury to do. Or they think they can't cook. They watch cooking shows and think it's only for the professionals. Everyone can cook. It's a skill, and like any skill, you can improve on it with patience and effort.

What if you make something that just doesn't turn out or taste good? Nice! How can you improve it next time? Add more or fewer spices? Alter cooking time? Ask yourself, what would make it better? Edison figured out ten thousand ways how *not* to make a light bulb. Similarly, you can figure out ten thousand ways how not to cook. All it takes is that one time to get it right, and then you can keep making it right.

If you don't like cooking often, try cooking on the weekends to prepare meals for the entire week, so that during the week, cooking is as easy as pressing the start button on the microwave. The only excuses are the ones you allow yourself to believe.

Changing your body weight does have to do with calories in versus calories out. If you want to lose weight, expend more calories than you take in. If you want to gain weight, take in more calories than you expend. It's simple math, really — except that it's not. Calories outside the body are not the same as inside the body. If they were, we would all have a near-perfect formula for losing or gaining weight. We all have different rates of metabolism, which affect how we use calories. I would recommend ignoring calorie counting, as it can become stressful and not worth the time. Use portions (a predetermined amount of food based on size) or the "Am I full?" test. Simply ask yourself, "If I stopped eating now, would I feel full?"

The most important tip I can give you is to listen to your body when you think you might be full. This new eating habit, along with daily exercise, had me lose twenty-five pounds in a little over a month. It's not easy, but tell yourself to wait ten minutes and then you can eat the rest of your food if you still feel hungry.

Also, it's okay to fail here and there when changing your habits! When some people go on a diet and they make a mistake (we all do at some point), it becomes an excuse to eat badly the rest of the day. Or, worse, they quit the diet altogether. So please be compassionate with yourself and allow yourself to make mistakes, because we all do.

Start with one of the habit changes above at a time, and work your way up until you feel as healthy as you possibly can.

Exercise:

When you start eating healthier, you'll start to get more energy, and when you get more energy, it's natural to want to use it. Exercise is not only great for using energy, it's also great for giving you more energy. When you exercise, your body feels more alive, more rejuvenated, and fresher to tackle the day's challenges.

Most people who want to start working out dread going to the gym. They say they're going to go, and then when it's time, they bail. This could be for multiple reasons, all of them excuses. Whether it's traffic, feeling lazy after work, "just not feeling it," or any other excuse, going to the gym is a chore for some people. When they go to the gym, their exercise strategy is often just the treadmill. They get on the treadmill, feeling out of breath almost immediately, and get discouraged.

I know, because that used to be me. Exercise shouldn't be a chore; it shouldn't be something you "have" to do. It should be something you *want* to do. If you don't want to do it, what makes you think you'll actually do it? I'm not talking about "feeling" like doing it, I'm talking about wanting to do it for yourself, for your health, and for your mirror of love.

If you actually want to work out, start by making your workout fun! If you like sports, join a local recreational league for adult sports or join a gym that has a basketball court. If you like to dance, join a dance class! Start with something that will make you excited about working out, and that will make working out fun. Then, as you get in the routine of enjoying exercise, start to integrate other kinds of workouts.

The best thing I found was P90X. I liked the idea of working out in my own home. I was afraid to go to the gym for fear of people making fun of me. I focused on whether other people were watching or laughing at me instead of on trying to improve. If that's the case for you, I recommend setting up a small personal gym in your house or apartment.

You don't need fancy equipment to work out at home, just some dumbbells or resistance bands and an area big enough to run in place. I also recommend searching for an on-demand workout-streaming service. There are many of them with thousands of workouts to choose from. Choose the one that's right for you, one that has workouts that you enjoy.

Also be sure to set fitness goals. Set goals for how many times a week you want to work out and what you want each part of your body to look like. Google images of body parts you like, cut their face out, print them and put them on your refrigerator so you remind yourself to eat healthy. I'm serious! If your goal is to lose twenty-five pounds, you'll probably weigh yourself every morning and could easily get discouraged with your progress.

Images are more motivating than numbers, so get excited about what you want to look like and go for it!

When you do complete a workout, make sure to get an ample amount of protein, ideally within at least an hour. The sooner after working out, the better. I like to drink a protein shake immediately after working out and then eat a meal an hour or two after my protein shake. If you skip getting protein in after a workout, you have literally wasted some of your time since your body won't recover to its full potential.

Nutrition and exercise are keys to a healthy, long-lasting life. Don't neglect them.

Flexibility:

I sometimes hear people say, "Yoga? No, not for me. I'm not that flexible." Isn't that more of a reason to do yoga? Some people think that you are either born flexible or you're not. Flexibility is something you work on, not something you're always born with. It's like lifting weights; the more you lift, the stronger you get. The more you stretch, the more flexible you get. Being more flexible helps prevent injury, makes you feel loose and relaxed, and leads to better performance and recovery.

Yoga is not the only way to become more flexible. Any form of stretching helps, especially if it's before or after a workout. If you're stretching before a workout, make sure to warm up the body with a jog or something to heat up your muscles. Never stretch a cold body.

Personally, I sometimes like to do a quick stretching session at night to relax the muscles before bed. I also tell my muscles aloud how much I love them while I do it, as strange as that may sound. Your body is always listening, whether you believe that or not. You move your body by thinking, whether consciously or subconsciously. Why would any of us think that *all* of our thoughts do not have an effect on our body as well? Positively or negatively, our body is always listening—just something to think about.

Whether or not you want to shower your body with love is up to you, but I do recommend having a healthy stretching routine somewhere in your day.

Good Posture:

Good posture not only helps build a confident appearance, but also helps you *feel* more confident. Posture is affected by how you sit, how you stand and how you sleep. If you do these three things with good posture in mind, it will not only make you feel and look more confident, it will also prevent a majority of aches and pains.

I often go to a chiropractor, and when I first did, I learned that my right leg was slightly shorter than my left. The chiropractor asked me if I sat with my wallet in my back left pocket. The small wallet affected my posture!

We don't realize how small a shift out of normal posture for prolonged periods of time affects how our body operates. One thing to consider is how you use your cell phone. If you are constantly looking down at your phone, you are putting almost ten pounds of pressure on your neck. I recommend going to a chiropractor, not just to get adjusted but to ask questions about how to develop good posture. You'd be surprised by how many people go there, get adjusted, don't ask any questions and keep doing the same things, so they have to pay to be adjusted again.

Showering:

Yes, showering is a skill. Did I mention everything is a skill? I thought so. Showering is how we keep our skin and body clean.

The best way to shower is with a loofah. A loofah is an exfoliating, sponge-like material that gets rid of all the dirty, dead skin off your body. I use it every morning in the shower. You start by wetting it first, then putting body soap or wash on top of it, and then wetting it some more. Starting from the area between your neck and your chest, firmly but gently scrub the loofah all over your body in a circular motion all the way down to your toes and the bottom of your feet. I also take the opportunity to tell every part of my body that I love it while I am using the loofah. Keep showering your body with love, literally.

While doing this, you are removing all the dead skin from your body, and if you consistently do this every day, your skin will feel more rejuvenated and more vibrant. Hooray vibrancy! If you are doing this in the morning, I recommend switching to a quick cold-water shower after you are done with the loofah. This closes up the pores so you can keep dirt and grime out of your skin all day long.

I know cold showers may not be all that fun, but they have so many other fantastic health benefits. They help with blood circulation and can help us lose weight as well. It doesn't have to be very long. Just rinse every part of your body with cold water so all of your pores close up.

As you can imagine, loofahs can get pretty nasty after removing all of that dead skin, so I recommend taking good care of them so they don't smell. After you are done soaping, clean out all the soap from the loofah, or it will start to smell, and then run them under hot water. After the shower, hang them up somewhere so they can fully dry after each use. Sanitize them once a week by putting them through the dishwasher, the washer, or boil them in hot water for a few minutes. Replace them every three to four weeks, and voilà! — you have learned the skill of showering. Now please go execute for maximum vibrancy. Hooray vibrancy!

Sleep:

The last component of your health is rest and recovery. How much sleep do you get? You commonly hear, "Get between seven and nine hours of sleep every night." But what if you have children with abnormal sleep schedules? Or what if you're an entrepreneur who's grinding to start a new business?

Most experts say seven to nine hours a night is optimal, but to me it all depends on your stress levels. More stress means more for the body to clean, and the more sleep you will need. It really depends on how you can mentally handle the daily challenges that life can throw at you.

Sleep is something you do when you need it. If you feel tired, then rest. Take a nap during the day. Re-energize yourself. If you're a mother, try to take a nap when your baby takes a nap, or when the kids are at school. If you're an entrepreneur, take a nap in between meetings or during slow periods during the day. Twenty to thirty-minute naps at a time is all you really need. Rest is crucial to being productive, being healthy and staying happy.

If you stay up all night binge-watching TV or playing on your phone, I absolutely recommend prioritizing more sleep. But if you can't do that, then sleep when you need it, and sleep when you can. If you have the chance to sleep ten or twelve hours one night after you've been grinding the previous week, do it! Your body will thank you.

You can also train your body to fall asleep more quickly. Eliminating caffeine after 2 p.m., not using your phone or laptop at least an hour before you go to bed, creating a bedtime routine that includes meditation, stretching, hot showers, relaxation and/or reading are all great strategies to go to sleep faster. If you have to use your phone or laptop before bed, dim the backlight as much as you can. The lights on screens can disturb your ability to fall asleep quickly.

Don't assume you need drugs to sleep. First try to do it naturally. Use medicinal drugs if you have to and if your doctor recommends it, but get the amount of sleep that works for you. Your physical happiness depends on it.

I put health skills first because our physical health has a lot to do with our levels of happiness. If we aren't physically happy, we can be cranky, fatigued, or uninterested in the beautiful things that go on around us. Setting a priority for our physical happiness creates a solid foundation for us to build our mental happiness on, which is what life is truly all about.

Loving Yourself/Others Skills: The skills for mental happiness

Changing Beliefs (Healing Insecurities):

If you can't change your beliefs to the ones you want, you'll never be able to love yourself or others. That is, you can't be habitually happy. The good news is that you *can* change your beliefs, with nothing more than patience and effort! (See below for developing those skills). Changing your beliefs involves repetition, emotions and awareness of thoughts. Most of your beliefs are subconscious; you have them instinctively. List the beliefs about yourself or the insecurities you have that cause you to hate any part of yourself that you want to change. Examples are: "I'm ugly." "I'm stupid." "My waist is not thin enough." "My nose is too big." "My boobs are too small." Whatever it is, write it down. If you have many, work on one at a time until you get the hang of it. Choose the belief you think will be easiest to change, or the one you want to change the most (i.e., the one that makes you feel the worst).

After you write it down, write on another piece of paper what you want to believe. Take the first piece of paper and either burn it (safely) or rip it up. This may sound silly, but it's symbolic of your letting go of the old belief. Now take the second piece of paper and write down the new belief ten times every day. Then read everything you wrote aloud every day with lots of emotion behind it. This may sound strange or not worth it, but it will literally take less than ten minutes of your time, and a lifetime of love heavily outweighs ten minutes a day.

It works best in front of the mirror. Starting with "I am" is where the jackpot is: "I am beautiful!!!" "I am intelligent!!!" "I am someone whose stomach is thinning through my new lifestyle changes!!!"

This may seem ridiculous at first, but do it for at least thirty days before you give up. Give it as much intensity and effort as you can for thirty days and watch your mirror of love get shinier and shinier. You may feel insecure doing it, but that's okay. Feel through your insecurity and do it anyway. That feeling will begin to fade, and it will be replaced with a new feeling of confidence.

Then, when you catch yourself thinking or talking about an old belief, quickly and without judgment, repeat your new belief aloud with emotion. If you are with other people, you can do it in your head — or you can be really committed to loving yourself and say it out loud. It helps if you have your new belief written on a note card kept in your purse or wallet. Then you can read it every time you catch yourself succumbing to the old belief.

With patience and effort you can accomplish anything, including changing your beliefs to love yourself completely.

Patience:

Patience is one of the best skills you can learn. If you can't learn patience, you will give up on the things that take time, and anything worth having takes time and trying your best — patience and effort. There is a reason they call patience a virtue. In a world of instant gratification, patience becomes a skill of the elite. So become elite, because you absolutely can.

Remember, patience is a mixture of relaxation and faith. It's being relaxed during a situation when things are expected to happen immediately, with the full faith that everything happens at the right time. You develop patience through situations that test your patience, particularly when you want things immediately.

In terms of loving yourself, when you are changing old beliefs, you may start to give up when it gets difficult. You may get irritated every time you repeat the new belief to yourself, because you might not yet believe it. That is being impatient. You're not going to believe it to be true until you put in the effort of reminding yourself every day that you are beautiful, intelligent and a masterpiece that is perfect, even with imperfections. Don't give up. Use those moments of irritation to calm the mind, reminding yourself that with patience and effort, you'll cultivate the mirror of love.

Every time you achieve that and keep doing the ritual of changing your beliefs, it's a huge mental win. Celebrate the mental wins! Give a nice Ric Flair "WOOOOOOO!!!!!" for yourself because you are starting to win. Celebrations lead to more celebrations, because your brain likes to be celebrated. And trust me, it deserves it.

Effort:

Effort comes from desire. You have to really want something. You aren't handed happiness; you have to earn it. As much as I wish we could all just sit on the couch and eat chips all day while watching reality TV and still achieve happiness, it's never going to happen. So cultivate desire. Desire always comes from a why.

Why are you trying to do this? Do you want to love yourself so you set an example for your children or for your siblings? Do you want to love yourself for the extreme amounts of joy, approval and happiness it brings you? Find your why; otherwise, you're building a house of cards that will collapse with one whiff of a breeze. Then link your why(s) and your desire to actions.

When you start to doubt or feel like giving up, remember your why! Write it down next to your new belief:

"I am beautiful because I am showing my kids that they are beautiful too."

"I am intelligent because I am a solution-finder and not a problem-starter."

The list can be long and the examples endless, but tie your why to your new belief and all of your actions. Then keep reminding yourself of your why, and keep putting effort into what you are doing.

Discipline (Following through on your commitments):

As Jim Rohn always used to say, "Affirmations without discipline is the beginning of delusion." The reason affirmations don't work for some people is that they don't have the discipline to continue doing them — or because their affirmation requires action, and they don't follow through with discipline.

Most people think of the word discipline as negative, given its other connotations. If that's the case for you, call it a commitment instead, because the skill of discipline in this context can dramatically improve your life in many positive ways.

Discipline is giving yourself a command and then following through. Like everything else, discipline is a skill we all can learn. Discipline is like a muscle: the more you exercise it, the stronger it gets. You may fail sometimes. You may fall off the wagon here and there, but get back on it. Just as lifting weights is designed to make your muscles fail, so too is exercising your discipline muscle. Work out, give yourself some rest, and then go back at it to get even stronger.

Jim Rohn gives this example: "Let's say I ask you to do as many push-ups as you can and the most you can do is five. It's clear that you gave it your all and that's the best you can do. But if you rested, you could do five more. Then if you rested some more, you could do ten push-ups. And if you kept going, you could end up doing fifty push-ups at one time."

This process is the same with discipline! Commit to something;

give it your all. Then, if or when you fail, give yourself some rest. Give yourself some space to relax — but don't stop too long. Rest should be a necessity, not the goal. Then go back at it vigorously! Keep trying to push yourself until you fail again. Then repeat. You'll notice that the periods in between failures will grow longer and longer.

The key to discipline is to start off by doing something you know you can do. You can't go to the gym and start by lifting fifty pounds of weights to get stronger—that only leads to injury, disappointment or giving up. Start with the weights you *can* do and work your way up. If you want to be healthy, but only think you can dedicate three days a week to exercising, start with three days! Discipline yourself to do what you think you can do, and when you have done it consistently, up the ante if you want to and do four days! If you struggle to do three days, try two days or maybe one day. Do that consistently and keep raising the bar until you have reached your goal. Take this example and apply it to other areas of your life you want to improve.

Discipline is what everyone means when they say "hard work pays off." Everyone wants to work hard—until it comes time to do it. As Denzel Washington once said, "Dreams without goals are just dreams, and they ultimately fuel disappointment. Goals on the road to achievement cannot be achieved without discipline and consistency." Without discipline, it can be hard to believe in ourselves, because we won't follow through on our commitments and our dreams, which will always fuel disappointment.

The beautiful thing about discipline is that more discipline in one area leads to stronger discipline in all other areas. If you discipline yourself with exercise, you'll have more of a discipline muscle to eat healthier, and so on. The stronger your discipline muscle, the more successful you'll be with your goals, and the more your life will positively change—guaranteed.

Confidence:

True confidence comes when you have complete faith in yourself. That faith is created when you have accomplished something or have learned something about yourself from your actions. Set a goal and go achieve it using discipline! Your confidence will start to soar. Every time you do that, you'll become more confident. Start with something that you know you can do but is also somewhat challenging. Exercise and nutrition are great places to start, but it can be any goal that causes you to take action, sometimes fail and then get back up, and learn something about yourself that you didn't know before. The beautiful thing about confidence is that when you gain more confidence in one area of your life, it carries over into other areas. If you gain confidence in your appearance, it can positively affect your finances, or the bedroom. You may still have to keep building upon it, but any growth in confidence is a win. WOOOOOO!

Also, don't confuse confidence with cockiness. Cockiness comes from thinking we are better than other people. It comes off as arrogant because it is, and people can see right through it. Arrogance is just an insecurity trying to hide itself. Cockiness gets swept away when someone calls us out or appears to do something better than we do. True confidence can't be shaken by anyone outside of us.

Open/Closed Mind:

There is a strategy to opening and closing your mind. If someone tells you about something you can't control, or makes you doubt or hate yourself, reject it immediately.

If someone tells you that you're ugly, stupid or worthless, reject that as a lie. First, those are their standards, not yours. Second, the person making the negative comment could just as easily see you in the opposite way, but instead lie to you to bring you down because they have low self-esteem. The only opinion that matters is your own. If *you* view yourself as any of those things, it's time to build the mirror of love.

Only open your mind to ideas that you can control and that can improve your life. If someone says something that is outrageous, but what they are saying has the potential to improve your life, don't reject it as false immediately. Give it some thought. Think about the possibilities it opens for you. You may want to research it more to see what other people have said, but you also don't have to take any action on it either. You may even decide later that it is total nonsense—but at least you gave it a chance rather than thinking you know everything. None of us know everything, so strategize what you open and close your mind to.

Forgiveness:

Forgiveness, like most things, is a process, not an event. You have to keep cultivating forgiveness for yourself and for others. If you don't, you'll be stuck with hatred and anger for the rest of your life, for no reason other than you can't let go. But you can let go. You have to in order to love — because your hate and anger hurt only you, especially if they're directed toward another person. It's not hurting the other person; usually they couldn't care less.

Forgiveness is about making the mental shift from blaming or hating someone (or yourself) for something that happened in the past, to letting go of what happened. You can't control the past; you can only control the present. When you start to feel that hate, tell yourself you forgive the offending person, or even yourself. What they did is a reflection of who they are, not who you are. Or, what you did is a reflection of who you used to be, not who you are now. If you feel remorse for something you did in the past, clearly you have changed into a better person. So take the lesson and learn to love yourself and the people who did you wrong. You'll know when you have completely forgiven someone when you can think of that person and not have any feelings of hatred.

I learned a trick from Sandy Gallagher. If it helps, you can start by thinking about someone you absolutely love. Feel the intensity of your love for them. Then, slowly put yourself or the person who is bothering you into your mind and continue feeling that love. Keep doing that until you have nothing but forgiveness and love for people who have done wrong to you, and you can wish them well to have peace and love in their hearts so that they treat other people better than they treated you.

Empathy:

The skill of empathy not only allows us to see things from other people's point of view, it also gives us a better understanding of why some people do what they do. This doesn't justify what they do, but it allows you to judge less and show more compassion for other people and what they are going through.

If you're complaining about someone, put yourself in their shoes, using all the information you have about them. If you know that their dad physically or mentally abused them, imagine if your dad physically or mentally abused you. How would that impact your life? Would you also be mean to others? If it's your boss, you may come to realize that they have many things to manage and get right. They probably also have a lot of pressure to succeed, and they might be taking that stress out on you.

Whoever it is, try to see things from their perspective. If it's a stranger, consider their appearance, body language and facial expressions. Put yourself in their shoes and see if you can somehow relate to them.

Compassion:

Once you are able to empathize with others, remember that feeling. Use it to show compassion toward them. If it's your boss, consider offering to help with something at work that you wouldn't normally be required to do. When you show people compassion and they feel that you are willing to help them, they naturally ease up a little. We all want to feel understood, and sometimes we lash out in anger when we don't feel as if we are.

Compassion is a mental skill. To learn self-compassion, when you start to beat yourself up for something you think you are not good at, become aware of it and understand that skills take time to learn. Then remind yourself that you are doing the best you can with what you currently know.

To learn compassion for others, when you start to judge someone, become aware that you are doing it and remind yourself that everyone has different backgrounds and lessons to learn.

Compassion is about being aware that you are judging or hating someone, or yourself, and then bringing yourself back to that feeling of empathy and understanding. Every time you do that, it's a mental win, and you'll find more peace in your heart.

Honesty:

Honesty is about always telling the truth and correcting yourself when you lie, but it's also about speaking your true feelings. If you're having problems with your boss, say something. Do it in a nice, friendly way that communicates, "I'm trying to get better at my job and make this relationship work." Do this with every relationship you have. Otherwise, don't complain about it!

If you're not willing to be courageous enough to be honest about your feelings, it's no longer the other person's fault. They may not even be aware of what they are doing or the effect it is having on you. I'm not going to say for sure that it won't end the relationship, whether it's with your employer, friend or significant other. But don't complain about it if you're not willing to try to change things. It's all about the way you approach your honest communication. If you go in with guns ablaze and start pointing fingers and blaming, it's probably not going to go well. If you can admit that you have some part in it from the beginning, it takes some pressure off of them, and they may be more willing to listen and perhaps change what they are doing.

First you have to recognize that it's possible that you might have been at fault in some way. Maybe you have been misinterpreting their communication. When you are honest about the possibility that you have a part in it, it eases the tension of being honest about your feelings with them.

Be honest about everything; otherwise, you have no one to blame but yourself if people keep doing things you don't like.

Kindness:

Kindness is about being nice to other people and to yourself. That's it. There's nothing fancy about it, but some people let their emotions interfere with their kindness. The skill of kindness is strengthened at times when your emotions want you to be mean or nasty. It's being aware that you are about to be mean to someone, and then switching to kindness instead. Or, it's a matter of recognizing that you have been mean to someone, then apologizing and offering them new words of kindness.

There will be times when you can choose to be kind or you can choose to be right. The ego wants to be right; your heart wants to be kind. When you argue with someone or think they are wrong, it's not going to change their mind unless you undeniably prove it to them. And even then, they're not going to think you're better because of it; they may even start to dislike you for shattering their pride. If it's something you feel strongly about, you can still be kind in showing them your way of thinking. Trying to make yourself seem smarter than others is never loving, but being kind always is.

Friendship:

Friendship is all about being there when your friend needs you. It's about dropping everything when the time comes to help. It's also about saying what your friend needs to hear, instead of what they want to hear. Of course it's about being kind to them, lifting them up, and encouraging them to be the best they can be, but it's also about pushing them when they get too comfortable or complacent. If they say they want to do something, encourage them to do it and help them believe that they can do it. When they give you the excuses for giving up, don't say, "Yeah, it's really tough. I would probably quit too." Tell them that they can do it and to keep going. Even if you think you would have given up already, don't let them give up. Keeping each other accountable, having fun with each other, and encouraging each other to believe in themselves is what friendship is all about.

Courage (Doing the Do and getting outside your Comfort Zone):

I wish I could say this was an easy skill to master. I've been learning it for more than a year and still feel that I haven't quite grasped it. Sometimes I crash through that bubble of comfort, and other times I'm afraid to keep going. But I haven't given up on learning it, and neither should you.

The first step is to recognize when you notice the nudge from within. Then, it's to do what it tells you as quickly as possible before your brain has time to make excuses. If you wait too long and you don't do it because of excuses (which are really just irrational fears), realize that it's okay. Be aware that fear is what stopped you, and that fear is something everyone experiences at one point or another. Then, next time, go for it. If you fail again, do it the next time. Eventually you'll do it, and the reward will inspire you to keep on doing it.

I wish fear didn't exist, but it does. Follow your heart in the face of fear, and you'll be so glad you did.

Gratitude:

Did you know that when you feel gratitude, you can't experience any other negative emotion at the same time? Gratitude is one of those emotions you can feel on command once you have practiced and learned it.

Gratitude comes when you start thinking about all the things in your life that you are happy to have. Think of all the things you sometimes take for granted. Maybe it's your car, clothes, food, water or even shelter. List all the things you are truly grateful for and are happy about having in your life. There are people who don't have those things — I mean even legs, arms, the ability to walk, or feed themselves. They live life without those things, so appreciate everything you have. What you appreciate, appreciates.

If you don't appreciate the things you have, why would you deserve anything more? Why do you think that having more will bring you happiness? Learn to cultivate gratitude for everything that makes your life better, especially if it's something you usually take for granted.

If you feel stressed, anxious or fearful, try pausing and taking a deep breath to clear your mind. Then think about the wonderful things you have in your life right now, and watch how your emotions shift from negative to joyfully positive.

Faith:

You always have faith in something. You could have faith in things always working out—known as optimism. Or, you could have faith that things will go in a negative direction — also known as anxiety.

Faith is a mental skill. It's not something some people have and others don't. Love and fear are at the opposite ends of the spectrum in life, so if you are constantly worried or anxious, it's impossible to feel love and happiness in those moments. Learning the skill of faith is vital to sustaining habitual happiness.

The skill of faith is developed in times where you feel anxious or worried about something. When you start to feel these emotions, become aware of it, and then change your thoughts to having faith in the universe, God, yourself, or whatever you believe in. Have faith that the answers will be provided, or have faith that you will figure out how to deal with whatever circumstances come into your life.

One trick is to take three deep breaths when you feel anxious. Breath in faith on every inhale, breath out fears on every exhale. You'll notice a sense of calm that wasn't there before.

When you develop faith in yourself, you will start to have the belief that you can handle anything — and beliefs define who you are.

Loving yourself and creating happiness is a process, not an event. Continually be building on these skills, and watch as your happiness becomes increasingly habitual.

Other Awesome Skills to Learn

Learning/Self-Learning:

Learning is all about finding the style of learning that works for you. Everyone learns differently. Some people are visual learners. Others are auditory learners. Then there are kinesthetic learners, who learn by doing. Most people learn from a mixture of all three, but tend to prefer one of the three. Figure out which way works for you. Remember: you can learn as much as you want, but without applying it, you'll only be an encyclopedia for other people to improve their lives, without improving yours.

Imagination:

Everything that has ever been created first appeared in someone's mind. The shirt you're wearing, the book you're reading, the bed, couch or chair you're sitting on were all first made in someone's mind. The iPhone was first created in Steve Jobs' mind before it came to life. The game of basketball originated in the mind of James Naismith. Engineers and architects first build buildings in their minds, then they draw them on paper, and only then do construction teams go out and make them. The mind is such a positive tool for creating.

What are you creating? Scenarios of anxiety, doubt and fear about things that don't exist? Your imagination doesn't care how you use it, it just always gets used. The mother who loses a child in the grocery store immediately jumps to the conclusion that the child has been kidnapped. Nine hundred and ninety-nine times out of a thousand, that's not what has happened, but the mother experiences the fear and anxiety as if it has happened until the child is found safe and sound. Many of us use our imaginations to conjure up the worst possible scenarios — and our brains can't distinguish real life from imagination. It makes you feel like you are actually living the fantasy you have drawn up for yourself. You've created terror for no reason, all because you haven't developed the skill of training your mind to imagine the best instead of the worst.

Focus on what you *do* want to happen. Maybe that single mother runs down the aisle and into a hot and sexy single man who has found her child and is trying to return them to their mother. Either way, the mother isn't going to stop until she finds the child. Perhaps instead of experiencing fear, she might experience excitement and joy at finding her child. It's all in your head.

When you notice you are imagining a scenario that makes you feel fear or anxiety, take control of what you want to happen. Experience the joy of what you want to happen instead of the fear of what you don't want to happen. If the worst case does occur (which it almost never does), deal with it then. But until you know for sure, don't create a false image that scares you when it probably won't even happen. Learn to take the bull by the horns and steer your mind in the direction you want it to go.

Listening:

Listening is a skill that most people have yet to learn. People hear what others say and then quickly think about how to respond with something they have experienced in their own lives. Most conversations consist of people going back and forth, talking about themselves. As much as you love to talk about yourself, other people don't actually care that much. They just want you to finish so they can talk about themselves. They may even interrupt you if you take too long. In a world where everyone wants to talk, being a good listener makes other people enjoy talking to you and may cause them to open up to you more.

If you want to develop deep, meaningful relationships with people, learn to be a good listener. Listening involves truly hearing what they have to say and thinking about what they have said instead of what you're going to say next. It's either asking questions about things you actually do want to know more about, or responding with an observation of how the reported situation may have made them feel. If it's a conversation with your spouse about his or her emotions during particular circumstances, then it's not just about repeating exactly what they said back to them. It's about truly understanding where they are coming from, asking them questions about what you don't understand, or repeating back to them what you think you understood in *your* own words, so that you both know you understood each other correctly.

You can learn a lot about a person's maturity based on how well they can listen. Learn to listen effectively, and watch your relationships and friendships start to strengthen.

Teaching:

Teaching comes from understanding that everyone has a different web of knowledge. Some people are better at certain subjects than others are. That doesn't make anyone smarter or dumber than anyone else. It just makes everyone unique, so your teaching style should be specific to the person you are trying to teach.

Ask how they learn best. If they don't know, that's the first thing you teach them. Then it's about catering to their unique style of learning, using patience, repetition and questions to gauge what they know, what they can improve upon, and where to go from there.

It really helps others learn more effectively if you can get creative, relating things through analogies. The more you do that, the better you'll get at it.

Reading:

Reading takes practice. If you're not a natural reader, that's okay! You can always learn how to read better by learning and practicing reading tips. Anyone can learn to read better than they do now, or even to speed-read. The only limitations are in your own head. Reading is good for the mind and makes you think. Don't give up on it.

Memory:

Everyone has a perfect memory. That's right; read that again. Your subconscious mind is basically a recorder, recording every moment of your life. It has recorded everything you have ever seen, touched, heard, smelled or tasted. This is why companies spend millions on advertising, because they know you'll subconsciously remember their commercial. Just because you can't remember all these things consciously doesn't mean your memory isn't perfect.

Bob Proctor talks about this all the time. If you put your right arm in a sling for six months while you lift weights with your left arm, your right arm will be weak, and your left arm will be strong. The same goes for your memory. When you practice using your memory, your conscious memory improves. But when you believe, “I have a poor memory,” you won’t even practice. You’ll just assume your memory is poor.

Memory is best built up through ridiculous association. That’s why Old Spice has the weirdest commercials. They know that when you’re shopping for body wash or deodorant, you’ll subconsciously be thinking of a blindfolded man swinging two tennis rackets on top of a whale that’s wearing sunglasses, or a man riding a horse backwards. Then you’ll consciously think of choosing Old Spice. Ridiculous? Only if you don’t know how memory works.

Earning Money:

There is an infinite number of ways to earn money. Learn a skill, or use one you already have, that will allow you to make money when you need it. It can be flipping things you find at garage sales online. It can be baking cookies and selling them at little league baseball games. Whatever your passion is, find a way to make money at it. It doesn’t have to earn you a million dollars or replace your primary job. Just find something that will pay off some small bills or allow you to have peace of mind if you find yourself in a jam.

Spending Money:

Learn how to spend money. Yes, spending money is also a skill. Create a budget and tell your money where it’s going. Don’t simply take your paycheck on a wild spree until it’s gone and you still have bills to pay. Be a master of your money, not its servant. There are lots of books on how to budget, get out of debt, and spend money wisely. I would read them so you have a better understanding of how you can use your money more effectively.

Saving Money:

Saving money is a skill. It just comes down to discipline. Tell yourself how much to save, when to save it, and what the money is for, and then follow through. Ten percent of your income seems like a good idea, but choose something that's right for you.

Please don't get overwhelmed by trying to learn all of these skills at once. Pick one or two to improve on first and go from there. Or pick some that you can practice at different times in your life or in your day, so it's not about learning different skills all at the same time.

Pick the ones that will make the greatest impact on your life right now. Only you know which ones those are. Don't feel like you have to master them; just improve on them day after day, moment after moment. When it feels right to add another skill, then do it.

There are many skills discussed here, but you have your whole life ahead of you. It's never too late to change your life. Even if you are sixty years old, with today's advancing technology, you could live for another forty years in great health. You're only as old as you think and feel you are. Start telling yourself that you are ninety-nine years young, and feel the youth and vitality that changing your words can bring.

Skillz pay the billz, so the more you learn, the more you earn.

RESOURCE 2

Definitions to Adopt

"We must think differently, look at things in a different way. Peace requires a world of new concepts, new definitions."

– Yitzhak Rabin, Former Prime Minister of Israel

This section is my "glossary" for the principal key words I use in life. As I said in the first chapter, because we all learn our vocabulary through context in conversations, rather than from a dictionary, we may have slightly different definitions of a word. I have adopted some of these definitions from others, and some are my own. I will give credit for other people's definitions that I've heard in parentheses. Some of these words may not apply directly to this book but can be used in other areas of life. If one of these definitions appeals to you, feel free to make it your own. Or, better yet, take my definition and improve upon it, molding it into what resonates with Who You Are.

Happiness:
The art of being yourself

Happiness comes from feeling love — mostly from loving yourself. In order to love yourself, you must be yourself in every situation. We all express ourselves differently in life situations, but this is about making sure that we express who we truly are in each of those areas. Otherwise, loving yourself is, in effect, loving an imposter — a kind of love that is impossible to sustain. Happiness is the result of doing what you love and doing things because you truly want to, not because you feel like you have to in order to gain an individual's or society's approval. So be the happiest you that you choose to be and find the love for yourself that you deserve.

Love:
A feeling that is a mixture of gratitude, happiness, and wishing well for others

Love is a hard word to define. The words in my definition above are the best I have found. If you love someone, you appreciate everything they do and that they are in your life—or even just alive. You're thankful for them, imperfections and all. You are also happy for them. No matter what happens in their life, if they are on a path to bettering themselves, you are happy for them. If they're happy, then you're happy for them. If they're clearly not happy or have hatred in their heart, you are wishing they can find happiness—that they can somehow transform their unnecessary unhappiness into the love we all deserve.

Approval:
My acceptance of behaviors and opinions on the basis of who I truly am, or by the people or groups of people who keep me accountable for what I say I want to be

Your approval is the only one that matters. If you must seek other people's approval, make sure it's because they are the ones who are keeping you accountable for what YOU say you want out of life. Strategize the approval you want from others and yourself, and your life will change forever.

Comparisons:
The thief of joy

It depends on how you do it, but comparing yourself to other people will likely steal the joy available in the present. That's true with anything: your relationships, your wealth, your skills and the like. If you want to focus on other people, focus on how you can help them or on how you also can do what they are doing.

Depression:
A sustained feeling of a loss of love

This can occur with grief-related depression due to the loss of a loved one, including from a breakup. But it can also occur when we make too many choices that leave us living a life we are not meant to live — a life we do not love. It feels as if there is no way out, so instead of fixing the cause, we sometimes mask the symptoms with drugs and alcohol. If you are experiencing depression, try to determine what's causing it. What about your life are you not loving? If you can acknowledge that some of your choices brought you to the place you are at, you can change the choices and your depression. Make different choices that take you somewhere new, where you can experience the joy and beauty life has to offer.

Anger:
A punishment we give ourselves for someone else's mistake (from an Instagram post)

Anger never solves anything. It only allows the target of your anger to win, because the anger is hurting you more than it is them. If you can learn to feel through your anger and eventually let it go, *you* win.

Forgiveness:
A shift in perception that removes a block in me to my awareness of love's presence (Mary Morrissey)

When you have hate for yourself or hate for others in your heart for something you or they have done, that hate blocks loving energy that could be your focus instead. We can't change the past, but we can change what we have learned from the past. Focus on what you have learned—and not exclusively on what happened — and your heart will fill with love and joy.

Comfort Zone:
A tight little bubble that keeps us in the same place

Comfort zones are where dreams go to die. They're where self-improvement and development are non-existent.

Intuition (The Nudge):
The still, small voice inside you that encourages you to do something different, but something that will be worth it

Your intuition may tell you to do or not do something. It nudges you to do something to make yourself better, or it tells you not to do something to protect you. Either way, it's always worth listening to.

Ego:
Insecurities that edge people out

Your ego is nothing more than the sum of all your insecurities. When you feel anger from someone hurting your ego, you can either heal the insecurity or you can edge other people out with your choices and actions.

Honesty:
Telling the truth, the whole truth and nothing but the truth

That is essentially what honesty is. It's also about correcting yourself when you lie, no matter how much time has elapsed since you told the lie.

Empathy:
The ability to put yourself in someone else's shoes and see life through their eyes

Seeing life through other people's lenses can have a profound effect on you. It will make you realize that your life isn't as bad as you may think it is, and you can learn to cultivate the wonderful emotion of gratitude for things you have in your life — whether that's love, joy, happiness, a car, food, clean water, shelter or anything else. Gratitude brings peace into your heart. When you practice empathy, you remain aware that everyone is dealing with something in life. Then being kind to them will come naturally.

Compassion:
Understanding that doesn't entail justifying

Compassion is the ability to understand that someone was born to love, and only later taught to hate. That hate and anger you see in someone else is something you can be grateful you weren't raised with, or that you have learned to turn that hate into love and peace. It's saying, "I am grateful for who I am and what I've learned, and I understand that this other person is on a path that will require learning these things too." However, compassion does not mean justifying the hate or anger. In this context, understanding and justifying are completely different. Understanding is knowing where the feeling comes from; justifying is deeming it acceptable. You can understand where hate and anger come from, love that person, wish them well to learn love and peace, and still denounce their behavior and actions.

Confidence:
The faith in one's ability to overcome obstacles through a process of accumulated successes and learning

Confidence comes when you believe in yourself. You believe in yourself when you have battled through challenges, experienced failures and kept going. It comes from knowing that you will get things done.

Positive Attitude:
A combination of positive thoughts, words and actions that are in harmony for purposes such as growth, solving problems and relentless persistence (Bob Proctor)

Your attitude defines your outlook on life. It also determines whether people want to be around you. Bob Proctor says your attitude is the composite of your thoughts, words and actions — and he's right. If you want a positive attitude, make sure that these three elements are harmoniously in sync to get what you want out of life. You choose all three elements, and they are quite possibly the only things you can control.

Integrity:
Doing the right thing, even when it might seem "hard," especially when no one is watching

Just because everyone is doing something doesn't make it right. You know in your heart what the right thing to do is, so do it. You've probably heard others say that your character is defined by the moments when no one is watching you. But it is also defined by the moments when you have the choice to speak up when you know that something is wrong, even if everyone around you is doing it. As Albert Einstein said, "The world is in greater peril from those who tolerate or encourage evil than from those who actually commit it."

Faith:
An unwavering belief in something

You can have faith in yourself or in someone else. It can also be in the fact that the universe always provides. What you have faith in determines your state of being. You can have faith that you can overcome anything that happens to you, and that it will lead you on a better path. That's called optimism. You can also have faith that everything that possibly can go wrong will go wrong. That's called anxiety. What you believe and have faith in defines who you are. Choose optimism and your state of being will help you soar past any obstacles.

Open Mind:
The ability to think about a new idea without immediately rejecting it

When you don't give new ideas a chance, you can't learn anything new. You can have an open mind or a closed mind to new things you hear about or learn. The trick is to think about the things that have the potential to improve your life and reject the ones that don't. If you think about a new idea and sincerely give it a chance, there is no harm in rejecting it later.

Success:
The progressive realization of a worthy ideal (Earl Nightingale)

Success is not a one-size-fits-all thing. One man's success is another man's nightmare. But I believe that this particular definition applies to everyone. It's moving in a forward direction, no matter how fast you are going, toward a dream or goal that is worthy enough for you to devote your life to it. In other words, success is about the journey to achieving your dreams, not about attaining the dream itself. Because once you attain a dream, it's on to the next one.

Problems:
Opportunities to grow

Problems aren't here to provoke us, put stress in our lives or make us feel weak or inadequate. Those are reactions we have to problems. We can just as easily look at them as opportunities to grow — chances to learn something new that will propel us forward positively into the next chapter of our lives.

Rejection:
Redirection (Jay Shetty)

Rejection is merely redirection. If you get rejected from a job, it is leading you to a better one. If you get rejected by a pretty girl or a handsome boy, it is leading you to a better one. Rejection redirects you to a better path — so let's be thankful for it.

Goals:
Specific, measurable, written statements of desired outcomes with an associated timeline

When speakers talk about goal setting, I usually begin to yawn. But a goal can be anything you want to achieve. We have goals every moment of every day, whether we have remembered to set them or not. Your goal could be to be entertained because you're feeling bored, so you begin scrolling mindlessly on social media. Goals steer your life in the direction you are going to go. When you want to go somewhere in your car, you have a goal — a destination of where you want to go. As the Cheshire Cat told Alice, if you don't care where you are going, it doesn't matter which way you go. The above definition for goals is how to set productive goals that steer your life in a positive direction. What goal you set is irrelevant; the goal isn't the point. It's who you become on your way to achieving the goal that matters. If you stake your happiness on the goal rather than the journey, the happiness of reaching the goal will last only a moment before it's on to the next goal. And if you don't reach the goal or give up, you give up on your happiness, too. When you find your happiness in the journey, that happiness becomes everlasting, and achieving the goal is just the climax, until it's on to the next one.

Sacrifice:
Giving up something of a lower nature to receive something of a higher nature (Bob Proctor and Mary Morrissey)

When people think of a sacrifice, they think of it as a bad thing. They think about it as if they are losing something, when really it's the opposite. You sacrifice doing something so that you can have, do or be more. Sacrifice isn't about losing something; it's about gaining something. What this means is that you can have conflicting goals at the same time. You can have a goal to lose weight as well as a present-moment goal of exploding your taste buds with chocolate cake. Sacrifice is giving up on your taste bud goal to achieve your health goal. In order to do this, you'll need the skill of discipline.

Discipline:

Giving yourself a command and then following through on it (Bob Proctor)

Discipline is following through on the commitments you make, both to yourself and to others. Discipline is a decision made in every single moment to either follow through on what you said you were going to do or not. You can say to yourself at the beginning of the week, "I'm going to work out every single day this week," but you still have to make the decision to follow through every day. When it's time to work out and you think of all the reasons you don't want to, that moment is when discipline must set in: "I don't care why I don't want to. I said I would, so I will." And then just go do it.

Forcing It:

Relentlessly trying to do something but insisting that it happens "your way"

Forcing things to go the way you expect or want them to always leads to disappointment and, possibly, the resentment of others. Persistence is important, but let's make the distinction between persistence and force. Force is like trying to put a huge truck tire on an SUV. It's not meant to fit there. That doesn't mean you shouldn't replace your tires; you just go about it a different way. People have an image of what they want out of their life, and they are 100% sure they know how to get it, until they fail. Forcing an outcome may bring success sometimes, but usually there is a much easier way that avoids frustration and anxiety. If you want to become financially free, does it really matter how you do it as long as it happens? When you're clinging to a business that will probably fail because you want to become financially free, that may be the time to give up on the business, but not the goal. Give up on forcing the method; persist on achieving the goal.

Persistence:

Trying to get something done without giving up

Persistence entails having your end goal in mind. It's not about getting it done a certain way, or "your way"; it's about getting it done, period. People try to force things that don't work, and instead of giving up on the method, they give up on the goal altogether. Never give up on the end goal. That may mean trying new ways to achieve it. It may mean starting over. Failure only happens when you quit on your dreams. If you never give up, you cannot possibly fail. KEEP GOING!

Frustration:

An emotion that is trying to tell you that you are either forcing something that is not meant to be, or that you are not doing what you should be doing

Frustration arises because you are either trying to force something to go the way you want it to go, or you are procrastinating to keep yourself busy instead of focusing on your goals. It may also come because you don't know your goals, so you don't know what direction to go in. Either way, when you experience frustration, feel through it and ask yourself why you are frustrated. Listen to your heart and adjust course in the direction you should actually be going.

Business:

A company whose purpose is to improve something, solve a problem or move humanity forward

The world doesn't need another fast food franchise or a new

company offering a different kind of toothpaste. It needs a fast food chain that offers healthy meals made from fresh, organic ingredients and a company offering toothpaste that comes in biodegradable or recyclable tubes. Businesses are made to help people in some form or another, not just to make a profit. Profits are necessary to sustain the business, as they're the fuel that keeps the engine going. But profits aren't the final destination. Purpose is, and that destination is always forward-looking.

Management:
The forward direction of people through teaching, learning, listening and making decisions to achieve a certain goal

When executives see their employees only as numbers, and therefore dispensable, employees see their executives and the company as a paycheck—and, well, also dispensable. People will do just enough not to get fired (i.e., the bare minimum), and they will leave the company when some other company offers them more money. People want to feel that they are more than just a number, that they are an important asset to the company. When managers and executives realize they are building a house, and their employees are the foundation, they'll put more time into building a strong foundation—a foundation that forms a bond between people working together for a cause that's greater than themselves.

Sales:
A set of skills and aptitudes that include listening to the customer, high enthusiasm for the product and/or service, confidence and a positive attitude

No one will buy anything from you if you wouldn't buy it yourself. You sell something to help a customer solve a problem or fill a need, not solely to make money. If you're focused on the money, the customer will know and most likely will not buy from you even if you can solve the problem. Listen to what they need or the problem they have, then figure out how to solve it with what you're selling—or move on to the next customer whose need you can actually fulfill.

Customer Service:

The ability to put yourself in the customer's shoes and see things from their point of view, usually through compassion and empathy

Have you ever been around someone you know should not be working in customer service? It's because they are focused on their own problems, and at the moment their problem is you. Customer service is about using empathy to solve a customer's need. Sometimes the customer isn't always right, but you won't know that until you put yourself in their shoes and feel what it is that they are experiencing.

Change your vocabulary, change your life — one word at a time.

RESOURCE 3

People to Learn From

"A mentor is someone who sees more talent and ability within you than you see in yourself and helps bring it out of you."

– Bob Proctor

When I started on my "Lone Wolf" journey, I did nothing but listen to motivational and inspirational YouTube videos. From when I woke up to when I went to sleep, I listened to some of the best speakers of our time talk about greatness. I started to follow them on social media, so my news feed was filled with positivity. Then I started adding positive, self-development books to my daily routine. I also joined a coaching program, attended a speech workshop and bought a course to help me become a better author. I wouldn't have gotten to where I am today without mentors. Mentors don't have to be people you personally know. They can be words in a book, a voice in your earbuds or a video on your phone. It is beneficial to have mentors you can talk to and who can help you through your current circumstances, but it's also good to listen to multiple people's point of view. It opens your mind to different ideas, and a range of new ideas can move your life in completely different directions. Listed in no particular order, here are some of the people I recommend listening to, reading about, and/or following on social media:

Gary Vaynerchuk (Gary Vee)

Gary Vee is a serial entrepreneur who preaches about posting content on social media. If you want to learn about entrepreneurship, social media marketing, branding or motivation to get what you want in life, this is your man. His messages include kindness as a business strategy, empathy as a way to ignore "the haters," self-awareness to follow what you want in life instead of listening to other people, and so much more.

Oprah Winfrey

Does she need a description? Her outlook on life is so powerful that it'll give you a boost of positivity just thinking about it. Check out her YouTube interviews and follow her on social media.

Tony Robbins

I'm not really sure how to describe Tony, other than to say he has the ability to disrupt the story people believe about themselves in a single moment. He has more than forty years of experience in getting people to act instinctively and without hesitation. He's a great source of information to obtain a different outlook on life.

Jay Shetty

He is a former monk turned entrepreneur with a mission to make "wisdom go viral." His social media videos are all about how to take the ancient teachings he learned as a monk and apply them to our everyday lives. He's a great source of modern wisdom.

Lewis Howes

Lewis Howes is an entrepreneur and social media inspiration, and he interviews some of the greatest minds of our age. He has a podcast called "The School of Greatness." If you want to fill your news feed with positivity, Lewis is a great place to start.

Mel Robbins

Mel Robbins is an author, television host, and the creator of the "five-second rule." The five-second rule refers to how long it takes your brain to start coming up with excuses after you've had the nudge to do the "do." She's an inspiration for anyone, but especially for women who have lived with the lies of insecurities the outside world has given them. With classic lines such as "Motivation is bullsh*t" and daily inspirational messages, Mel is a must-follow on social media.

Tom Bilyeu

Tom is an entrepreneur and host of the YouTube series "Impact Theory." Like "The School of Greatness," "Impact Theory" is a series of interviews with some of today's most fascinating people, mainly in video rather than audio format. Tom does an excellent job of asking questions to engage the interviewee and get the most out of them. In addition to "Impact Theory," he takes a hardcore philosophy toward life that he shares with his followers. If nothing else, Tom is honest about what he believes. Check out his social media pages if you want to learn more about what he has to offer.

Bob Proctor

If you have an open mind, look up Bob Proctor. Bob has a phenomenal view of life and has been studying personal growth and development for almost sixty years. If you listen to Bob without an open mind, you might think he's crazy, but, more times than not, he's preaching the truth. Just because you don't understand something doesn't make it false. If you decide to listen to Bob, bring an open mind, a pen and a notepad, because your way of thinking will surely change in a very positive, life-changing direction.

Dr. Joe Dispenza

Dr. Dispenza is an educator and lecturer who teaches the science behind changing your life. He uses the field of quantum physics to explain things such as how you can get your body to heal itself, and the science behind the way changing your beliefs can change your life.

Les Brown

Les Brown is a motivational speaker. He often says that believing he could make a million dollars was far harder than actually making the million. Les, who has a twin, grew up with the belief that he was dumb. He was labeled educable, mentally retarded, and kids at school called him "the DT" — the dumb twin. It wasn't until he started spending time with and listening to successful people who believed in him that he was able to believe in himself. His speeches will inspire you to take action, so I suggest looking him up on YouTube. Also, if you have an event at which you need a speaker, consider Les.

Jim Kwik

Jim is a learning guru. Once labeled "The Boy with the Broken Brain," Jim turned his childhood head injury into determination to learn how to learn. He now teaches people how to memorize, speed-read and how to learn more quickly. Jim is also an extremely humble guy, which is the icing on the cake. If you want to learn how to learn, see what Jim can teach you.

Simon Sinek

Simon is an author whose dream is a world in which everyone goes to work fulfilled. With principles and books such as *Start*

With Why, Leaders Eat Last, and *The Infinite Game,* Simon is disrupting the ways businesses view how their employees should show up to work every day. Simon is also someone whom I try to model my style of selling after. Instead of using manipulations to get people to make immediate purchase decisions, such as "Buy now and you'll get a discount," "Here's the value of what you're getting, but if you buy today it's only this price," and all the other tricks of the trade companies and individuals use to get you to buy something, Simon teaches how to build loyal customers. In a world in which you can buy anything from anyone, loyalty is really what matters most.

Dr. Carol Dweck

Dr. Carol Dweck is the founder of the growth mindset. She discovered that the belief that one can get better at any particular subject causes people to actually put the effort into learning more about that subject. A fixed mindset, the growth mindset's opposite, makes the claim that knowledge and learning are fixed, and that there is no room for improvement. If knowledge is fixed, why try? Effort is obviously the key to growth. Without the belief that your effort will pay off, you won't try in the first place. Many people have expanded on what Carol has discovered. Learn about and develop a growth mindset, and watch your life change forever.

Peggy McColl

Peggy McColl is an author's dream mentor. She knows how to turn books into best sellers, and I went to learn from her to help write this book. If you want to be an author, I highly recommend you look her up.

Bill Gove

Bill Gove is said to be the father of modern day speaking. His system for speaking has been used by Zig Ziglar, Brian Tracy, Bob Proctor and many others. Unfortunately, he is no longer with us, but his workshops and principles are taught by Steve Siebold and his lovely wife Dawn, who ran a speaking business with Bill. I have taken the workshop and can personally say that it was one of the best workshops I have ever been to. If you want to earn money speaking or learn how to become a better speaker, this workshop is the place to go.

Dalai Lama

If you want to see someone who is at total peace, start listening to the Dalai Lama. His social media accounts are probably not his own, but the messages are the same as if he had typed them himself. He follows the belief that compassion for all is the only way to make this world a better place, and he's right.

Jim Rohn

Jim Rohn was a motivational speaker whose speeches remain on YouTube. Almost everything he talks about is pure gold. If you want to get serious about personal development, I highly recommend listening to this man.

Albert Einstein

Albert Einstein is most famous as a genius in the world of physics, but I think he was also a genius in the world of life. Look up some of his quotes. Don't just read them; think about them to discover their true meaning. Everything he said has far more weight than it appears at first glance, so try to understand the meaning behind what he has said and written.

Buddha

Buddha has taught me the value in monitoring my thoughts. Our thoughts have more power than we think, especially with regard to happiness, health and even wealth. Buddha's teachings about settling the mind down, controlling how and what we think and directing positive, loving energy toward ourselves and others are why I think the Buddha is worth studying.

Jesus

Then there is Jesus. It doesn't matter if you are a Christian. Believing that Jesus is the Son of God isn't a requirement for learning from his teachings. He taught that God, the universe, our creator, Allah, or whatever you choose to call the source of all things loves each of us unconditionally. Jesus also loved everyone unconditionally. Love Everyone Always is the true inspiration from his teachings. He didn't teach Love Everyone Always because he thought he was the only one who could do it. He showed us this so that we learn it for ourselves.

If I have left out someone you think is important, feel free to add them to your list, but these are the people I know of and have had a significant impact on my life. Some of these people have conflicting views, and I personally don't always agree with everything they all say. The point is not to agree with everything you hear, but to learn new ideas that resonate with who you are. Take the beliefs and ideas these people share, keep the ones that resonate with you, and discard the others. Either way, learning is never-ending. Whether what you are after is money, a loving relationship, a fulfilling career or everlasting friendships, the more you learn, the more you truly earn.

RESOURCE 4

Recommended Reading

"Reading is to the mind
what exercise is to the body."

– Joseph Addison, Poet

Think and Grow Rich
By Napoleon Hill

This book has made more millionaires than any other, and it really has nothing to do with money at all.

Conversations with God
By Neale Donald Walsch

This book will challenge your way of thinking about who and what God really is. This book has completely changed my life and allowed me to forgive myself for many of my wrong doings. You'll learn a lot about life in this book, but please come with an open mind.

The Power of Your Subconscious Mind
By Joseph Murphy

This book has also completely changed my life. After reading and listening to it, the same will happen to yours if you trust Mr. Murphy.

Start With Why
By Simon Sinek

A new way on how to market, sell, and direct companies to be bigger than just making a profit. A must-read for anyone who wants to start a business or learn the skill of marketing and sales.

The Soulful Art of Persuasion
By Jason Harris

This is the new *How to Win Friends and Influence People.* It teaches you how to persuade without giving up on your soul. In fact, it teaches you how to use your soul to persuade.

Rich Dad Poor Dad
By Robert Kiyosaki

A new way of looking at how money can work in your life.

The Total Money Makeover
By Dave Ramsey

Looking for a get-rich-quick scheme? Don't buy this book. Dave teaches how to build wealth the real way: with patience and effort. Discipline will be required to achieve the Total Money Makeover, but the steps he lays out aren't complicated. They're only difficult because they make you alter your financial behaviors.

The Four-Hour Workweek
By Tim Ferriss

If you're looking for a new way of living, this is your book. Tim challenges you to use the Pareto 80/20 principle to get more done in less time, and to set up your life so you can enjoy "mini-retirements" instead of waiting until you're old to enjoy the freedom of retirement.

Psycho-Cybernetics
By Maxwell Maltz

This book is written by a plastic surgeon who noticed that some patients changed their self-image after plastic surgery, and others didn't. It wasn't the plastic surgery that determined how people viewed themselves, but rather it was the idea they had formed in their minds about who they are. If you want to learn more about creating the mirror of love, this is a great book.

The Science of Getting Rich
By Wallace D. Wattles

Much like *Think and Grow Rich*, this book shows you how to get truly rich without even talking about money management. If you approach it with an open mind, this book may change how you view the world around you.

Untamed

By Glennon Doyle

This book is about how society has conditioned women to live in a certain way, mainly to put everyone else's needs above their own. This book is a must read for every woman (and really every man) to help women get their happiness and power back.

Made in the USA
Coppell, TX
29 May 2021

56508575R10125